PRICE LEVEL REGULATION FOR DIVERSIFIED PUBLIC UTILITIES

Topics in Regulatory Economics and Policy Series

Michael A. Crew, Editor
Graduate School of Management
Rutgers University
Newark, New Jersey, U.S.A.

Previously published books in the series:

Rowley, C., Tollison, R., and Tullock, G.:
  Political Economy of Rent-Seeking

Frantz, R.: *X-Efficiency*

Crew, M.: *Deregulation and Diversification of Utilities*

Shogren, J.F.: *The Political Economy of Government Regulation*

PRICE LEVEL REGULATION FOR DIVERSIFIED PUBLIC UTILITIES: AN ASSESSMENT

Jordan Jay Hillman
Northwestern University
School of Law

Ronald R. Braeutigam
Northwestern University

Kluwer Academic Publishers
Boston/Dordrecht/London

Distributors for North America:
Kluwer Academic Publishers
101 Philip Drive
Assinippi Park
Norwell, Massachusetts 02061 USA

Distributors for all other countries:
Kluwer Academic Publishers Group
Distribution Centre
Post Office Box 322
3300 AH Dordrecht, THE NETHERLANDS

Library of Congress Cataloging-in-Publication Data

Hillman, Jordan Jay.
    Price level regulation for diversified public utilities : an
assessment / Jordan Jay Hillman, Ronald R. Braeutigam.
        p.   cm. — (Topics in regulatory economics and policy series :
5)
    Bibliography: p.
    Includes index.
    ISBN 0-7923-9028-8
    1. Public utilities—Rates—Law and legislation—United States.
2. Public utilities—United States—Rates.   I. Braeutigam, Ronald.
II. Title.   III. Series: Topics in regulatory economics and policy ;
5.
    KF2103.H55   1989
343.7309'1—dc20
[347.30391]   89-34144
                                                           CIP

Printed in the United States of America

Contents

Foreword and Acknowledgements

This book is the final product of a research project sponsored by the Corporate Counsel Center of the Northwestern University School of Law. The project was funded through a 1985 grant to the Center by American Information Technologies Corporation (Ameritech). The principal condition of the grant was that it be used to support research in regulatory matters. Within this broad purpose, the particular subject matter was determined by Professor Hillman, of the Law School, as principal researcher and Professor Braeutigam, of Northwestern's Department of Economics, as economic consultant. These authors appreciate the support provided by Ameritech's grant to the Center and the complete independence accorded to them in their work. They also wish to acknowledge the substantial contributions of Messrs. Erik F. Dyhrkopp and Steven M. Spaeth, as law student research assistants.

A further condition of the grant was that the final results be presented at a Law School conference. This was held on November 18, 1988. Following the principal presentation by Professors Hillman and Braeutigam, responsive commentaries were made by two academic economists and two academic lawyers. The economists were Victor P. Goldberg, Thomas Macioce Professor of Law, Co-Director, Center for Legal and Economic Studies, Columbia University School of Law and Almarin Phillips, John C. Hower Professor of Public Policy and Professor of Law and Economics, University of Pennsylvania. The lawyers were Ian R. Macneil, John Henry

Wigmore Professor of Law, Northwestern University School of Law and Richard J. Pierce, Jr., George W. Hutchison Professor of Law, Southern Methodist University.

The inherent complexities and tensions of price level regulation, whether for diversified or non-diversified public utilities, were underscored in these responses. The Afterword to the book contains a brief summary of some of the major points made by three of the commentators. Professor Macneil preferred not to have his views stated in summary form.

PRICE LEVEL REGULATION FOR DIVERSIFIED PUBLIC UTILITIES

Introduction and Statement of Purpose

The limitation of natural monopoly revenues through cost based rate of return (or, as used here, "profit level") regulation is widely viewed as a source of productive and allocative inefficiency. Assuming for the moment a sound basis for such views, the need remains for some manner of public intervention to constrain the potential abuse of private economic power in natural monopoly markets. Among the alternatives under consideration is price level regulation. Its essence lies in the unlinking of the firm's allowed revenues from its actual internal costs.

The principal potential gain from such unlinking is the elimination of the prime disincentive to productive efficiency under profit level regulation—its central focus on the equating of total costs (as derived through regulatory processes) and revenues in inelastic markets. Under price level regulation, in place of indirect price limits resulting from direct constraints on cost based revenue levels, revenues in the regulated market would be a mere consequence of controlled *maximum* prices (or "ceilings"). *In theory, if the desired utility output could be achieved at lower total costs, with consumer prices at least no higher than those which would have prevailed under the former regulatory regime, social gains would be realized in the natural monopoly market.*

In providing service in relatively inelastic natural monopoly markets, diversified public utilities increasingly operate as well in both regulated and unregulated competitive markets.[1] Accordingly, the calculus of potential gains and losses from price level regulation must include its impact on these markets.

A central problem associated with public utility market diversification under profit level regulation has been the firm's incentive to effect cost transfers from relatively elastic competitive markets (whether or not regulated) to relatively inelastic regulated markets. Under such regulation, however, efforts to constrain intermarket subsidies regularly run afoul of the Scylla of structural separation or the Charybdis of stringent cost allocation controls. In the former case the efficiency benefits of economies of scale and scope may be largely or wholly denied. In the latter case, inherently arbitrary allocation standards can generate equally arbitrary prices justified neither by actual costs nor demand conditions.

Active consideration of the price level regulatory alternative has thus far largely occurred within the telecommunications industry. Concern for competition in unregulated markets has figured prominently in the deliberations. New technologies within the industry have had the greatest impact in (i) opening to seemingly viable competition markets traditionally viewed and regulated as natural monopolies and (ii) spawning new competitive markets functionally related to, or dependent on, the provision of regulated telecommunications services. The proliferating market complexity of telecommunications firms has spurred new efforts to control, or reduce, their normal incentives under profit level regulation to overallocate joint and common costs to regulated natural monopoly markets.

At the federal level an impetus for regulatory consideration of price level regulation came from the favorable July 17, 1987 recommendations of the U.S. Department of Commerce, National Telecommunications and Information Administration ("NTIA").[2] There followed in August, 1987 the Federal Communications Commission's ("FCC") rule making notice for the use of "price-caps" in lieu of profit level regulation for "dominant" carrier markets. These included the interstate interexchange services of American Telephone and Telegraph Company (AT&T) and the interstate *carrier* access services of local exchange carriers.[3] Reduced reliance on cost allocations to control the firm's incentive to cross subsidize was cited by both NTIA and the FCC as a potential major advantage of price level regulation.[4] By its Further Notice in May, 1988 the FCC invited comments on a specific proposal to establish a voluntary "price-cap" regime for both dominant carrier categories.[5]

Emergent state regulatory interest in changing the focus of regulation from profits to prices is reflected in such developments as (i) a 1987 Vermont enactment permitting negotiated contract prices "for basic exchange telecommunications service" and (ii) an aborted proposal in Oregon for implementing by administrative rule a voluntary price level regime for "local exchange [telecommunications] services."[6]

These various price level proposals for the telecommunications industry are rooted in the model provided by British Telecommunications plc ("British Telecom"). In 1984 this majority investor owned regulated firm took over the newly privatized telecommunications assets and operations of the British Post Office.[7] In rejecting the profit level regulatory model, the British government chose to regulate the firm's prices directly through a license formula limiting annual aggregate increases (at least until July, 1989) to the annual change in the British Retail Price Index minus a 3 percent productivity factor ("RPI-3").[8]

While a special interest in price level regulation in the telecommunications industry was stimulated by its growing market complexity, equal impetus came from the desire for improved productive efficiency in its natural monopoly markets. This latter goal is no less relevant to the basic residential and commercial markets of electric, natural gas and water utilities.

The purpose here then is to consider price level regulation for the natural monopoly markets of diversified public utilities in this broader context. This consideration will include both issues of productive efficiency in regulated markets and of allocational efficiency among markets. Chapter 1 presents a survey of the most widely perceived defects of current profit level regulation and their impact on diversification, as measured against relevant economic standards. Chapter 2 discusses the welfare implications of the revised entrepreneurial incentives under price level regulation and of the major decisional issues involved in the establishment of a price level regime. Chapter 3 begins with a brief summary of the potential benefits of price level regulation and proceeds to discuss the problems it presents. Chapter 4 offers several suggestions for use in implementing a price level regime for diversified public utilities.

1

The Inefficacy of Profit Level Regulation for the Natural Monopoly Markets of Diversified Firms

A. AN ECONOMIC OVERVIEW

1. Economic Rationale for Regulation

The first question in any assessment of current or alternative forms of regulation is: "Why regulate at all?" From an economic perspective[9] the classic basis for regulation has been described as follows: "The most traditional economic case for regulation assumes the existence of natural monopoly—that is—where economies of scale are so persistent that a single firm can serve the market at a lower unit cost than two or more firms."[10]

Even as the efficacy of the expanded scope of modern regulation has been increasingly questioned, this seminal point continues to find widespread support: If an industry is a natural monopoly, it can be served at a lower cost by a single firm than by any industry configuration involving two or more firms.[11] If an industry is truly a natural monopoly, there is not room enough for competition within the market.

Important revisions in economic thinking, however, have contributed to the view that regulation of natural monopolies may not always be warranted on economic grounds. Contemporary literature on regulation suggests that there may be at least three ways to introduce competition into a natural monopoly market. These are (1) franchise auctions, (2) contestability, and (3) monopolistic competition. If such competition for the market can be introduced successfully, then regulation may be avoidable and efficient resource allocation may be achieved even under conditions of natural monopoly. The three models are considered in turn.[12]

First, even if competition *within* the market is not possible, there might be competition *for* the market through an auction for an exclusive franchise.[13] Under such competition excess profits would be bid away and a firm would have incentives to minimize production costs.

The franchise auction, however, has been seriously questioned. The outcome is in effect a contract between a franchisor (a governmental authority) and a franchisee (the firm winning the competitive bidding). As such it naturally gives rise to many of the problems discussed in connection with the design and enforcement of contracts.[14] Since the franchisee might well adopt the short run strategy of providing the lowest quality service possible once it has won the right to serve, the franchisor will have to specify minimum quality standards for the service to be provided. There is no guarantee that administratively determined minimum service standards will provide "optimal" resource allocation. It may also be difficult to incorporate contractual procedures for price and quality adjustments to changing market conditions. And finally, while the notion of a winning bid may be well enough defined for a single product market, the determination of a winner in a multiproduct setting may be difficult. No one firm is likely to be low bidder on all required services, and a suitable weighted average may be difficult to calculate and administer.

Competition may be possible without a formal auction if the market is "contestable". A contestable market is one in which both entry and exit can occur in a costless, frictionless manner because of the mobility of all factors of production.[15] A firm may enter a market and compete at whatever price it wishes. If it exits the market, it can recover the full value of its assets through sale or transfer to another market. In other words, there are no "sunk costs" associated with entry into a market.[16] If a number of firms with identical technologies are contemplating entry into a contestable natural monopoly market, the surviving firm will earn normal (but not extranormal) returns on investment, just as under a franchise auction. Any firm attempting to set prices that would yield extranormal profits would be driven out by another firm charging lower prices. These conditions will encourage the existing "monopolist" to respond to potential competition in contestable markets as if it were actual competition.

One advantage of contestability over a franchise auction is that it can be implemented in a multiproduct setting (but only in the absence of sunk costs). A second advantage is that a contestable market requires no issuance and oversight of an exclusive franchise contract. Conversely, a major advantage of the franchise auction is its applicability to industries with sunk costs.

The third form of possible competition is so-called "monopolistic competition".[17] This involves competition among similar but differentiated products. If the rivalry is strong enough, it may induce firms to produce efficiently and prevent the earning of extranormal profits. A prime example is found in "intermodal competition" among railroads, motor carriers, pipelines, and water carriers, all of which compete for freight traffic. Such competition among different, but functionally similar, products or services is often cited as a basis for deregulation in freight transportation (most notably the railroads), even where a particular transport mode appears to have the cost structure of a natural monopoly.

Given these theoretical possibilities for competition, the question remains: "Why regulate a natural monopoly?" First, it may not be feasible in particular natural monopoly markets to introduce competition by any of these means. Moreover, even where one or more of these means are feasible, a further case for regulation may exist. Regulation may allow for pricing schemes more sophisticated than those which are feasible under a franchise auction, contestability, or monopolistic competition. Such pricing schemes may improve resource allocation significantly beyond what is possible under competition for the market. In such cases regulation may be useful even where competition for a market exists or is possible.[18]

2. Economic Goals of Natural Monopoly Regulation

Consider the case of a natural monopoly market which is to be regulated either because competition for the market is not possible or, if possible, would lead to less efficient resource allocation than under regulation. What are the commonly identified economic goals of such regulation? While the following list is neither exhaustive nor mutually exclusive, it should prove useful in assessing the performance of both profit and price level regulation.

One basic economic goal of regulation is the economically efficient allocation of resources (e.g., maximizing the sum of consumer and producer surplus, a rather standard measure of net economic benefit).[19] The major elements of surplus maximizing regulation include the first six points listed below.[20]

(1) **(Efficient Input Choice):** The regulatory constraint should induce the firm to produce output in a way that minimizes production cost. Resource allocation will be efficient only if the firm produces at minimum cost. In particular, the regulatory regime should not create an incentive to waste resources in an attempt to maximize profits (whether in the form of a return on an excessive rate base or managerial perquisites).

(2) **(Economic Viability):** As long as it is possible under some pricing scheme for the firm to cover its costs, then it is socially beneficial for the service to be provided. Regulation should therefore allow the firm to remain economically viable, so that the regulated service continues to be provided.

(3) **(Efficient Output Choice):** The regulatory constraint should induce the firm to produce outputs at economically efficient levels (i.e. at *total* surplus maximizing levels.)

(4) **(Incentive to Innovate):** The regulatory constraint should provide an incentive for the firm to engage in beneficial innovation. Such innovation would include cost reductions over time as well as the introduction of new services and products the value of which exceeds costs.

A significant regulatory complication results from a firm's diversifying into a competitive market. For the purpose of later comparisons of profit and price level regulation under such conditions, consider a simple form of diversification. Assume the regulated firm contemplates diversification into a competitive market currently served by a number of other firms. Thus, in entering the market the regulated firm would not be able to affect the market price of the competitive service. Assume further that the demand for this competitive service is unrelated to the demand for the monopoly service provided by the firm. In such case the following two goals for an economically efficient regulatory scheme may be stated.

(5) **(Incentive for Economically Efficient Diversification):** The regulatory constraint should be structured so that the firm has an incentive to diversify into a competitive market only where such diversification is economically efficient. Conversely, the regulatory regime should not deter welfare maximizing diversification.

(6) **(Marginal Cost Pricing in a Competitive Market):** Where the regulated firm diversifies into a competitive market, it should produce in that market at the level that price equals marginal cost.[21]

In pursuing efficiency goals, regulators, of course, cannot ignore equity considerations. A regulator will necessarily seek to protect the consumers in the monopoly market from any adverse effects of diversification into competitive markets. The regulator may therefore impose a kind of "stand alone test" to ensure that consumers in the regulated market will not be worse off with than without diversification.[22] This possible regulatory objective can be summarized as follows.

(7) **(Equitable Treatment):** Customers in regulated markets should pay a price no higher under diversification than they would be required to pay if the firm were prohibited from entering the competitive market.

(8) **(Implementability):** Regulatory rules should be structured so that enforcement depends only on observable, verifiable operating and accounting data for the firm, such as information on revenues, output levels and total expenditures. While the regulator might prefer to include other data within the enforcement mechanism, such "discretionary" data may be subject to manipulation or misreporting by the firm.

3. Incentives Under Rate of Return Regulation

Since the seminal work of Averch and Johnson (A-J),[23] research emphasis in the economics of regulation has emphasized the kinds of economic inefficiencies created by regulation. The economic literature has focused on how traditional regulatory constraints induce profit maximizing enterprises to misallocate resources, contrary to the central regulatory goal of replicating competitive conditions.

The term "rate of return regulation" has been used in the literature to encompass a number of types of regulation. The Averch and Johnson model investigates the behavior of a profit maximizing monopolist operating under a rate of return on investment constraint. A key assumption in the analysis is that the allowed rate of return exceeds the actual cost of capital. If the allowed return equals the cost of capital, the model degenerates.[24]

It is not necessary to explore the Averch-Johnson model at length here. It is noted that under this model (assuming its validity) five of the regulatory goals identified above are not achieved. First, when the allowed rate of return on capital exceeds the actual cost of capital, a profit maximizing firm will operate with a ratio of capital to labor which is too high to minimize costs in producing any observed level of output. This is the essence of the well known "A-J effect". It suggests that the firm fails to achieve the first listed goal of efficient input utilization.

Second, the firm can not be induced to produce on an inelastic region of demand, even if production in that region is economically efficient.[25] As a regulator lowers the allowed rate of return toward the actual cost of capital, a lower price may result. However, at least in theory, the firm may intentionally raise its input costs to avoid having to lower price to the point of operating on an inelastic region of demand. Contrary to goal (2), the model therefore indicates that the level of output chosen under rate of return regulation proves inefficient.

Three additional failures of rate of return regulation occur where a regulated firm serving two markets, one competitive and the other a monopoly, operates under a rate of return constraint on the combined markets. Under the same assumption that the regulator sets an allowed rate of return exceeding the actual cost of capital, Averch and Johnson point out that a firm (contrary to goal (6)) might have a long run incentive to price below long run marginal cost in the competitive market. Although the firm runs a loss from the increased output in the competitive market, the expanded activities in that market increase its rate base. The firm is then able to raise its price in the monopoly market to earn the allowed return on the larger rate base. If the increased revenues in the monopoly market more than offset the losses encountered in the competitive market, sales at a price below long run marginal cost in the competitive market will be profitable. This may make it possible for the regulated firm (contrary to goal (7) to use monopoly market revenues to "subsidize" ventures into competitive markets.

Averch and Johnson suggest that in some circumstances a firm might pursue this strategy until the price of the monopoly service under regulation reaches the same level that would prevail absent regulation. Contrary to goal (5), therefore, in these circumstances diversification into a competitive market may be profitable for the firm in cases in which diversification is otherwise inefficient.

Problems posed by the Averch-Johnson model of rate of return regulation are best understood as possibilities rather than as realities. The literature is filled with objections to the formulation itself, ranging from mixed support for the model in empirical tests[26] to the form of the model. For example, it is questioned whether allowed rates of return do normally exceed the actual cost of capital.[27]

Where rate of return regulation is applied to monopoly markets only (to the exclusion of diversified competitive markets) the degeneracy of the rate of return model disappears when the allowed rate of return is equal to the actual cost of capital. Assume the firm serves markets with both relatively inelastic and elastic demand and the regulator seeks to protect customers in inelastic markets. These are designated as "core" markets and made subject to a revenue constraint. The relatively elastic, or "noncore", markets are freed from such constraints. This would accord with the normal expectation of consumer protection in monopoly markets in which the firm has substantial pricing power and the deregulation of competitive markets in which the firm has little or no power.[28]

The demands for the core and noncore markets are independent of one another. The noncore market is perfectly competitive, so that the regulated firm acts as a price taker in that market. The firm incurs two kinds of costs: (i) those easily identified with and assignable to individual services and (ii) those joint or common to two or more services, and thus not easily assignable to individual services.

Consistent with the general practices of regulatory agencies over the past two decades, it is assumed that the regulator will attempt to determine which portions of the common costs of the enterprise should be assigned to individual monopoly services and which portions to individual competitive services, using a "fully distributed" cost pricing scheme to determine revenue requirements in specific markets. The portion of common costs allocated to the monopoly service is assumed to increase as the relative level of output in that market increases, and to decrease as the relative level of output in the competitive market increases.[29] A rate of return constraint is then applied to the core markets, requiring that the revenues generated in a core market cover all of the costs allocated to that market (including capital costs, reflected in an allowed return on investment). This approach contrasts rather sharply with the highly aggregated model of Averch and Johnson, in which a single rate of return constraint is imposed on the entire enterprise.

Contrary to goal (5), this form of cost based regulation may render diversification unprofitable, even where socially desirable. The outcome depends on the method of allocating the common cost of the enterprise to the individual services. Contrary to goals (3) and (6), if the firm does diversify, it may be induced to underproduce relative to the efficient output level in the competitive market. The reason for this is that as the firm increases the level of output in the competitive market, its profits are affected by two factors. First, in the competitive market, the incremental profits are affected by the difference between price and marginal cost. If this were the only effect on profits, the firm would expand output to the economically efficient level at which price and marginal cost were equal. But there is a second effect. As the firm expands its competitive output, a smaller portion of common cost is allocated to the monopoly market. This further limits the amount of revenue that the firm may earn in the monopoly market. Accordingly, it provides an incentive for the firm to produce less in the competitive market than would be economically efficient.

Profit level regulation also presents problems of reporting incentives and implementability, contrary to goal (8). In practice the regulator often depends on the firm for cost information, including a classification between assignable and common costs. If the regulator relies on the firm for the determination of cost categories, then incentives to misreport arise. As long as this form of cost based regulation imposes a binding constraint, the firm will have an incentive to maximize the portion of costs allocable to the core services.[30] In turn, this incentive will often stimulate regulatory overreaction through constraints contrived to minimize the amount of costs that the firm may recover in the monopoly market.

As for cost reduction incentives, contrary to goal (4), these prove strongest in the noncore market and weakest in the core market. This occurs because an actual dollar cost reduction in the noncore service (i.e., the market in which the firm is a price taker) increases profit by a full dollar. However, the same cost reduction in the core service results in a reduction in the revenue requirement in that service. The firm will still have some profit incentive to reduce attributable costs in a core service where (i) more service is demanded as price falls and (ii) price exceeds marginal cost. But the profit incentive to engage in such cost reducing efforts diminishes as the regulatory constraint becomes more binding.[31]

Two additional potential problems with profit level regulation can be identified. First, it may deter economically efficient diversification. If the projected regulatory allocation of common expenses to the core market is inadequate, the firm might choose not to diversify in order to avoid a substantial revenue reduction in the core market(s). In such case the benefits of economies of scope from diversification would be lost.

The second problem arises from possible market misclassification, as where a highly competitive market is erroneously classified as a core market and all core markets are placed under a single revenue constraint. The firm might then have an incentive to expand production in the competitive "core" service to a level at which the market price is below marginal cost. The incentive would be provided by an increase of expenses allocated to the core market group based on relative output or attributable costs. In turn the overall revenue allowance for core markets would increase. This could prove profitable for some range of production at below marginal cost in the misclassified competitive "core" market.[32]

B. A LEGAL OVERVIEW

1. A View from the MFJ:
A Selective Approach to Intermarket Subsidies

A general skepticism about diversification underlies Judge Harold H. Greene's formulation and administration of the Modified Final Judgment ("MFJ") in AT&T's divestiture proceeding.

> The more the Regional Holding Companies diversify, the less central their telecommunications functions will obviously become to their corporate existence. To the extent that these companies perceive their new, unregulated businesses as more exciting, or more profitable than the provision of local telephone service to the American public—as they obviously do—it is inevitable that, should they be permitted to embark upon such business enterprises on a significant scale, their managerial talent and financial resources will be diverted from the business of providing such service. As a consequence, both the quality and the price of that service are bound to suffer.[33]

His more specific concerns relate to intermarket subsidies and their dual impact on regulated rates and unregulated competition.

> As long as a Regional Holding Company is engaged in both monopoly and competitive activities, it will have the incentive as well as the ability to "milk" the rate-of-return regu-

lated monopoly affiliate to subsidize its competitive ventures and thereby to undersell its rivals in the markets
where there is competition. For that reason, caution with
respect to "outside" activities is always warranted, particularly in the case of wholesale diversification because the
larger the scale and the greater the diversity of a company's
activities, the more difficult it is to detect and to remedy
cross subsidization between the various affiliates.[34]

Under profit level regulation the incentive to generate "favorable" intermarket transfers is in fact shared alike by diversified firms
and their regulators. The regulatory pursuit of social or political objectives will often result in the calculated use of "benign" subsidies.
A notable example is the regulatory use of "yellow page" advertising
profits to support local exchange telephone operations.

The effort began with the rejection by Judge Greene of the initial
consent decree proposal by AT&T and the Department of Justice to
bar the Regional Bells and their operating subsidiaries from the "yellow page" market. A major consideration for him was the general understanding "that the Yellow Pages provide a significant subsidy to
local telephone rates [which] would most likely continue if the
Operating companies were permitted to continue to publish the
Yellow Pages." In turn, "The loss of this large subsidy would have important consequences for the rates for local telephone service."[35]

In a subsequent ruling, Judge Greene prescribed conditions
under which these operating companies might obtain waivers from
the initial decretal ban on diversification.[36] These included the requirement that unregulated operations for which waivers were granted be conducted through separate subsidiaries. Most, if not all, of the
Regional Bells then sought to place their directory advertising operations in separate unregulated subsidiaries. The aim was to insulate
the profits of these unregulated operations against their use as offsets to revenues otherwise recoverable through local exchange rates.

State regulators were less moved by considerations of structural
symmetry than by the consequential loss of substantial unregulated
revenues. In a typical response, the Arizona Corporation
Commission simply imputed to the revenues of the local exchange
carrier the $43 million in profits realized by the separate corporate
operator of the "yellow pages".[37] The regulatory appropriation of
these profits from unregulated markets is rationalized as a contribution to the widely supported social goal of more affordable basic telephone service. The point at which political goals are pursued under
the guise of social goals is, of course, difficult to discern.

2. A View from the FCC:
Cost Allocation and Transfer Pricing

In similar vein, recently promulgated FCC cost separation rules operate to effect cost transfers from regulated to unregulated markets.[38] These rules were developed as part of a continuing FCC process of lifting the structural separation requirements imposed initially on pre-divestiture AT&T, and later on the post-divestiture Regional Bells as well, for the provision of unregulated enhanced services and equipment.[39] With the exception of so-called "average schedule" carriers,[40] the separation rules are also applicable to other local exchange carriers.

In a "Summary" of its Initial Report and Order, the Commission posited as the "ultimate statutory objective" the promotion of "just and reasonable rates for services in the interstate jurisdiction." More to the point, its aim was "...to develop a system of accounting separation that would inhibit carriers from imposing on ratepayers the costs and risks of unregulated ventures."

The rules cover both intracorporate transfer pricing and the allocation of non-assignable common expenses. As for the former, different requirements are applied to asset transfers *to* and *from* regulated services. In the absence of a prevailing price list, intracorporate or affiliate asset transfers *to* regulated services are priced at "the lower of their cost to the originating activity... or their fair market value." Conversely, asset transfers *from* regulated accounts to intracorporate or affiliate transferees are determined "at the higher of cost...or fair market value...."[41] The consistent aim in either case is to reduce the regulated rate base or the amount of recoverable operating expenses.[42]

In justifying the differential treatment, the FCC conceded that it would not view negatively the rule's discouragement of some affiliate transactions. If the rules did have such "an adverse affect on potential transactions, we believe that, on balance, prevention of cost shifting is the more important goal", considering that "(I)mproper pricing in affiliate transactions is a classic and difficult problem of rate base, rate-of-return regulation." As an alternative to the use of affiliate suppliers, often at lower cost, the FCC posited "purchasing from a third party."[43] The imprimatur of the FCC has encouraged the adoption of the same rules by state regulators.[44]

The FCC rules covering the allocation of common costs show a similar bias toward cost reduction for regulated services.[45] Based on a "fully distributed costing methodology" ("FDC"), the rules set out broad standards for allocating residual common costs (i.e. other than directly assignable costs). On their face, these general standards ap-

pear to define a neutral analytical process. They call for: (i) direct
analysis of cost origins; (ii) indirect, cost-causative linkage to directly
assignable cost categories and (iii) a general allocator based on the
ratio of all expenses directly assigned or attributed to regulated and
unregulated activities.[46]

Inevitably the ambiguities and complexities of these guidelines
will spawn the usual prolonged controversies as firms strive to maximize, and the FCC strives to minimize, the costs allocated to regulated activities. Apart from these broad contentious procedures,a
separate and more specific rule applies to the allocation of investment in "central office equipment" and "outside plant". The allocation of these significant investment categories between regulated and
unregulated services are to be "...based upon the relative regulated
and nonregulated usage of the investment during the year when
nonregulated usage is greatest in comparison to regulated usage during the three consecutive years following the effective date of the current annual access charge filing." (Emphasis added.)[47]

This final rule on reconsideration modifies the original proposal
by changing the relevant time period from "the average life of the
plant" to a three year forecast period. Also in contrast to the final
rule, the "Summary" of the initial order preceding the actual text of
the rules sets out the following contradictory allocation principle:
"Telecommunications plant cost categories will be apportioned based
on relative demand at the point during the average life of the plant
in the category when demand is expected to peak."[48] In the end the
FCC chose not to apply this principle of relative usage at total peak
demand to these major investment categories. Its aim again is to reduce the regulated rate base and to allocate the largest possible cost
and risk to the unregulated use of the joint and common facilities. In
all, the rules suggest a present potential for regulators to manipulate
costs at least equal to that of the regulated firms.

3. A View from the States: Transfer Pricing

Purchases by a regulated utility from an affiliated supplier pose
the most common form of transfer pricing. Since the utility's payout
is to an affiliated interest, the major importance of the transfer price
to the combined corporate entity is the cost recorded in the utility's
regulatory accounts. The utility will benefit from recording the highest possible (or plausible) purchase cost for supplies or investment
value for capital assets. As demonstrated in the FCC's transfer pric-

ing rules, the utility's desire to record the highest cost is met by the regulator's desire to record the lowest.

In general, the principal transfer pricing standards for which the various interests may contend are (i) actual cost to the affiliate-transferor, excluding any return (aka "no profit to affiliate" rule); (ii) actual cost to the affiliate *including* a return on affiliate investment limited to the utility's allowed return; (iii) actual cost to the affiliate including a return based on some normal return realized by firms comparable to the affiliate in its industry sector; and (iv) the prevailing market price, as determined by arm's length commercial sales of the same product by the affiliate, or of the same or a comparable product by other firms.[49]

Whichever of these substantive standards may prevail in any particular transaction, the administrative procedures for dealing with the problem can be burdensome. The governing statutes of Illinois, Minnesota and Pennsylvania reflect the general pattern.[50] All three jurisdictions require prior submission and approval of any contract of significance with "any affiliated interest". In none of these jurisdictions does approval of a particular contract, with or without prices included, bar the regulatory agency from later questioning the reasonableness of transfer prices under the approved contract.

The substantive statutory provisions vary slightly in verbiage, if not real content. In Minnesota and Pennsylvania the public utility is expressly required to provide satisfactory proof of the cost of the services or property supplied. In any contested proceeding it assumes a broader burden of proof to establish "the reasonableness of the contract" (Minnesota) or that payments do not exceed a "reasonable price" (Pennsylvania). The Illinois statute applies an equally broad "public interest" standard, but without explicit assignment of the burden of proof.

The Illinois statute also contains a remarkable provision which underscores the potential for transfer price regulation to foster inefficiency. For whatever reason, the legislature was prompted to bar the Illinois Commission from *requiring* a public utility to purchase at a *higher* price from a non-affiliate supplier solely on the grounds that the proposed *lower* price charged by the affiliate yields the affiliate a rate of return in excess of that allowed the public utility.[51]

The fluidity of the standards governing inter-affiliate transfer prices is suggested in three separate decisions involving the purchase of coal by Montana-Dakota Utilities from its wholly owned subsidiary, Knife River Coal. The differing treatment of the coal transactions between the same parties arose from the operations of the utility in North Dakota, South Dakota and Montana. All three rate case decisions involved the transfer price allowance for purchased coal.[52] In general, Montana-Dakota bought from between 33 and 45% of Knife River's output. The balance of its output was sold competitively to other buyers.

In North Dakota the State Supreme Court reversed a commission decision which, in effect, imputed $40,000 in revenues to the utility representing the "excess profit" which the commission claimed the affiliate had realized from the relevant sales. The basis for the commission's finding of this amount of "excess profit" is not disclosed in the court's opinion, nor was it crucial to its decision. The court justified its "fair market value" standard by the identity of prices paid by the parent utility and all other buyers from the subsidiary. In the circumstances of these substantial commercial sales, the court held that "...the profits of the company's non-utility business are of no concern to the Commission."

In South Dakota, under essentially the same circumstances, the commission rejected the use of fair market value. Instead it established a transfer price principle which limited the subsidiary's return from the relevant sales to that allowed the utility. A majority of the South Dakota Supreme Court accepted excess profits rather than fair market value as the proper standard, but reversed the commission. The determination of excess profits was to be made with reference to returns realized by five independent coal companies. The dissenting chief justice would have used fair market value as measured by the affiliate's substantial commercial sales at competitive prices.

In Montana the commission found the competitive market for the affiliate's coal sales was insufficient to permit any determination of fair market value. It then limited the affiliate's return to that allowed the utility. The Montana Supreme Court chose not to impose either a rate of return or fair market value methodology. It did, however, fail to find "a factual reason for the summary rejection of the marketplace cost of coal approach...." It also rejected the limitation of the affiliate's return to the utility's allowed return, noting that any limit on rate of return should be based on the "comparable marketplace" rather than "a pre-determined rate... for a regulated utility." In remanding the case, the court observed that "As a matter of justice...it might be better for the PSC to use a marketplace cost of coal approach...rather than using the rate of return method with all of its difficult theories and computations."

Ultimately, a divided Montana Supreme Court, despite its apparent preference for a "marketplace" approach, affirmed a commission order based on a rate of return methodology.[53] By this time 75% of

Knife River's sales were in competitive markets, with only 25% sold to its parent at competitive prices.[54] Nevertheless, the commission compared Knife River's most recent *overall* return of 22% with an average 15% return earned by six natural resource companies which sold coal and oil. It then reduced the utility's coal purchase allowance to a level which, at 100% of sales, would generate the 15% return.

Thus we have three jurisdictions with three varying or vacillating sets of Commission/Court views on transfer pricing applicable to essentially the same transactions. These varying standards in themselves, however, do not begin to describe the complications (to which the Montana Supreme Court refers) of applying rate of return regulation to the operations of the affiliate supplier.

The welfare issue in transfer pricing will often boil down to efficiency incentives. Where prices are judged by rate of return rather than fair market value standards, the efficiency benefits of lower costs are taken from the utility enterprise, the actual source of the efficiency, and transferred to its consumers. Once again, the utility's incentive to productive efficiency is eroded. The essence of the problem is captured in the following passage from a state regulatory decision:[55]

> As compared to the independents, CSSC [the affiliate] was able to make its sales with fewer operating expenses, smaller accounts receivable, and generally fewer assets. Therefore, while the commission concedes to the company's assertion that the transfer prices charged by CSSC are equal to *or less than* the prices charged by independent distributors, it is apparent to the commission that CSSC does not incur the same level of operating costs. The commission concludes that in a regulated environment a reasonable transfer price is one that is based on the supply affiliate's cost and fair and reasonable return on equity, and not solely on a price level charged by nonaffiliated wholesalers who deal in a competitive market. (Emphasis added.)

4. The Uses and Abuses of "Stand Alone" Costs

If diversified utilities and their regulators were angels bent on achieving total objectivity in intermarket cost transfers, the cost distortions of profit level regulation would remain. The arbitrary character and economic irrelevance of the FDC methodology has been summarized by a U.S. Court of Appeals.[56]

As for arbitrariness:

First, FDC is a quite arbitrary allocation of costs among different classes of service. There are countless FDC methods, each allocating costs by a different mathematical formula.

As for economic irrelevance:

FDC cannot purport to identify those costs which are *caused* by a product or a service, and this is fundamental to economic cost determination.

In its initial proposed rulemaking notice covering cost separations the FCC indicated its intent to retain its traditional FDC allocation methodology.[57] It did so while fully recognizing that its prodigious pursuit of a suitable FDC formula in Docket 18128 "...did not produce lawful rates." Instead, "...the procedures were so unwieldly and complex, and the data they produced so massive and incomprehensible, that this Commission was unable to prescribe lawful rates to replace the rates we found unlawful."[58] Nevertheless, the FCC again rejected the economically preferable alternative of a marginal cost methodology. Its principal ground appears to be that "...marginal cost standards, however attractive in theory, are difficult to use for regulatory purposes because marginal costs are not readily measured by conventional accounting methods." Given the practical difficulties in determining marginal costs, a question arises as to whether "stand alone" costs offer a more suitable cost related benchmark less subject to the manipulative opportunities offered by FDC methodologies.

Stand alone costs for a market or a set of markets are commonly defined as those costs which would be incurred by a hypothetical efficient entrant into (in this case) a regulated monopoly market or set of markets.[59] The related stand alone cost test is used solely to define ceilings, or maximum revenue levels, in those markets. This test reflects a theoretical view of an industry with economies of scope and scale derived from joint or common costs: i.e., that the revenue contribution from consumers in a protected regulated market is not excessive if not above the level of costs at which a potential entrant would find entry into the particular market or set of markets advantageous. The test is not appropriate for determining either rate floors or specific rate levels. In simply defining a theoretical maximum for revenue contributions from regulated markets with inelastic demand, it differs in usage from FDC which is regularly used to set floors, ceilings and specific rates.

As a standard for determining appropriate cost ceilings, stand alone costs are theoretically superior to FDC. Whatever the difficulties of calculation, the concept offers an unambiguous theoretical benchmark.[60] In contrast, the FDC "model" is fraught with ambiguity. It is essentially devoid of any theoretical basis for *a priori* distributions of joint and common costs.

Because of the theoretical appeal of stand alone cost analysis, a different literal meaning of the term is often applied to profit level cost determinations. *Particular cost categories* in the regulated market are determined on a so-called "stand alone" basis in lieu of costs actually incurred in the regulated market by virtue of the overall structure of a diversified firm. Such selective usage, however, is subject to the same result oriented manipulation as transfer pricing and FDC cost allocations.

Where this version of "stand alone" deprives the regulated operations of shared cost benefits, regulators and consumers will *ordinarily* oppose its use. They will instead support a cost analysis that maximizes the benefits realized by those operations from joint and common, or pooled, costs. Conversely, they will *ordinarily* support "stand alone" where lower regulated market costs result. The issues of tax expense and capital costs illustrate such usages.

In determining rates for interstate pipelines, the FPC originally derived the expense allowance for federal income taxes from the system's consolidated return. Consolidation was used by the parent to realize an immediate benefit (rather than a more speculative carry forward benefit) by applying the tax losses of some of its entities against the current tax liabilities of others. For rate making purposes in these circumstances the FPC allocated any net tax loss of the combined unregulated entities among the regulated entities proportional to their taxable income. This formula ordinarily reduced the allowed tax expense.

In *FPC v. United Gas Pipeline Co.*[61] the U.S. Supreme Court considered the regulated pipeline's objections to the failure of the FPC to make full allowance for its "stand alone" tax liability. In affirming the FPC, the court observed that "Rates fixed on this basis would give the pipeline company and its stockholders not only the fair return to which they are entitled but also the full amount of an expense never in fact incurred. In such circumstance the Commission could properly disallow the hypothetical tax expense...."[62]

In its 1972 *Florida Gas* decision the FPC reversed itself and based the tax allowance on the taxable income of the separate pipeline.[63] Its initial rationale for this policy shift drew heavily on the need to encourage exploration and development by both regulated and unregulated affiliate producers. This purpose would be better served by not using losses in other markets to lower the rates and revenues of affiliated regulated pipelines.

Within a year, however, in *Southern California Edison* the FPC extended the new methodology to the wholesale rates of an electric utility to which the exploration and development rationale had no application.[64] This ruling drew on the "alternative ground for decision" in Florida Gas "...that utilities should henceforth be considered as separate entities for the ratemaking purpose of determining their costs...."

In *City of Charlottsville v. FERC*[65] the city, as appellant, challenged the "stand alone" methodology as applied to Columbia Gas Transmission and Columbia Gulf Transmission, subsidiaries of Columbia Gas System.

Notwithstanding the Supreme Court's dicta in *United Gas*[66], the D.C. Circuit Court properly considered its holding as permissive rather than mandatory. It then affirmed FERC's application of its "stand alone" policy.

In the same proceeding, however, the Court accepted FERC's contrary treatment of capital costs. Here, the court noted, FERC "...uses the capital structure *and capital costs* of the parent, Columbia Gas System, Inc., to determine the pipelines' rates of return." (Emphasis added.) FERC's decision did have a practical foundation. First, the parties had initially agreed to such usage. Further, the court accepted FERC's finding that "(N)othing in the record establishes that use of the pipelines' own capital structure and costs would have produced a lower rate of return." Finally, the Court agreed with FERC that "...even if the pipelines' 'actual' capital structures and debt costs yielded a lower return, the Commission was under no obligation to use them."

The court's reference to the pipelines' "actual" costs, however, seems misplaced. "Actual" in this context is best understood as their existing capital structure and interest costs, as determined by the parent. As such, they represent neither the specific risk based rate of return nor the debt/equity ratio of a "stand alone" pipeline.

If FERC's stated policy (as announced in *Florida Gas* and *Southern California Edison* and applied in *Charlottesville* to the tax issue) is to consider each regulated utility as a separate entity,[67] then the determination of the capital costs of that utility in terms of its specific risks is a critical component of the policy. The risk of a single interstate pipeline may well vary from the combined risk of a holding company system comprised of 7 major distribution units, 3 other pipeline units, 3 natural gas exploration and development units and diverse unregulated units.[68]

Where the pipeline enjoys a stable and diverse customer base its separate market risk could be lower than that of a more diversified natural gas system operating in higher risk markets. This possibility could explain the willingness of the pipelines in *Charlottesville* to "concede" the use of the parent's overall risk in determining their capital costs.

In *Charlottesville*, FERC in fact claimed the inclusion of capital costs within its stand alone policy.[69] As it explained, however, its consideration of rate of return begins with a presumption that the parent's capital structure and costs are appropriate for the regulated subsidiary, subject to any necessary adjustments duly established by the parties. In this proceeding the pipeline had stipulated to the use of its parent's capital structure and costs (as had Charlottesville, to its ultimate regret).

Unless FERC's experience indicates that pipeline risks are normally comparable to system risks, its presumption of identity is unwarranted. A more consistent application of a stand alone policy would call for an affirmative effort to determine pipeline risks and capital costs in each major rate proceeding. The circumstances suggest, however, that FERC's overriding concern was for the financial viability, or general well being, of the natural gas industry. To that end it was prepared, as required, to use or avoid, if possible, the "stand alone" rule.

Under state regulation the general effort is made to determine separately the capital costs of regulated utilities operating as holding company subsidiaries or as parents of regulated or unregulated subsidiaries. In the case of holding companies, this effort commonly involves the imputation of a capital structure other than that chosen by the parent. The rationale for the practice arises from the parent's use of funds derived from debt for equity investments in subsidiaries. The subsidiary may then contend for a higher rate of return based on the higher cost of equity capital.

The intended effect of the imputed "stand alone" capital structure is to reduce net capital costs through the lower cost and interest deductibility of debt.[70] Once a "stand alone" approach for determining capital structure is adopted, logic compels the determination of a hypothetical return based on the risks associated with the separate regulated entity. Since the utility's equity is wholly, or largely, owned by the parent, market data offers little direct help in determining its actual equity costs. Accordingly, their determination must rely even more heavily on such generally established analytical techniques as discounted cash flow, capital asset pricing model or comparable earnings. The process rarely breeds certainty. As indicated in the cited cases, the hypothetical equity costs of a subsidiary are often more speculative and subject to manipulation than those of the publicly owned parent.[71]

Where the desired result requires inconsistency in the use of a "stand alone" approach, state regulators are equal to the task—even where the "stand alone" calculation presents no great difficulty. Thus, Alascom, Inc. is regulated by the Alaska Public Utilities Commission as a wholly owned telephone subsidiary of Pacific Telecom, Inc. This parent has various ownership interests in over 50 corporations, consisting of interexchange and local exchange telephone companies, cable television operators, unregulated telecommunications services and realty. Pacific Telecom, itself, is an 87% owned subsidiary of PacifiCorp, also the parent of numerous other subsidiaries.

In determining Alascom's capital costs the Commission constructs a hypothetical capital structure based largely on comparability standards. It also determines a separate cost of equity, with primary reliance on discounted cash flow. Having applied these "stand alone" techniques to its capital cost determination in a particular rate case, the Commission in the same proceeding rejected the principle by requiring use of the system's consolidated tax liability to reduce the allowable tax expense of the regulated utility. To do otherwise, in its view, would be "...inapposite to the basic philosophical premise underlying the consolidated tax approach which is to reflect no more than *actual* cost in revenue requirement."[72] (Emphasis added.)

In general, state regulators show understandable concern for insulating utility consumers from the possibly greater risks of diversification. This is reflected in their usual efforts to identify the specific risks and capital costs of the regulated component. Occasionally, however, diversification will have clearly succeeded in lowering the diversified firm's overall risk and capital costs. In such case the regulator will abandon stand alone capital cost analysis in order to capture the benefit of lower system costs for ratepayers. *Washington Util. and Transp. Comm. v. Pacific P. & L. Co.* is an example.[73]

In determining the cost of equity, the Commission accepted the views of an expert witness who selected "comparable" companies "...with the purpose of matching Pacific's actual [i.e. not separately determined] cost of equity so as to share with ratepayers any reduction in the cost of equity caused by diversification."[74] This reflected the policy (endorsed by the Commission) that "...the regulated utility has an obligation to lower its costs through diversification if it may do so."

The "logic" which seeks to insulate consumers from diversification risks while assuring them the benefits of its reduced costs is a natural consequence of profit level regulation. It typifies the issue of the extent to which the efficiency benefits of diversification must be allocated to consumers in the regulated market as a political condition of diversification.

5. Regulating the Structure of Diversified Utilities Under Profit Level Regulation

The ultimate structural control over cost transfers between regulated and unregulated markets is the prohibition of the regulated firm's existence as part of a diversified enterprise. The restrictions on diversification under the MFJ have been noted.[75] That these were directed mainly to competitive, rather than regulated, market concerns is indicated in the stated basis for the possible future lifting of the restrictions. Any waiver would require a showing "...that there is no substantial possibility that [a local exchange carrier] could use its monopoly power to impede competition in the market it seeks to enter."[76] Notably absent in this rationale was any express reference to the possible impact of diversification on costs and prices in the regulated markets. That reference is found in a later dictum that "...the objectives of affordable rates and universal service...complement the goal of an industry free from anticompetitive action, and they thus mirror the prohibition on cross-subsidization."[77]

In the end, Judge Greene's decisions are unclear on the relative weight given to the impact of diversification on competition in unregulated markets and on costs, prices and service quality in regulated markets.[78] Accordingly, how the replacement of profit level by price level regulation might affect his views on diversification into telecommunications related markets is conjectural.[79]

In its concern for competition in unregulated telecommunications related markets, the FCC's focus has shifted from structural constraints to cost allocation and equal access rules.[80] Accordingly, the Public Utility Holding Company Act ("PUHCA") remains the principal area of federal regulation pertinent to the relationship between industry structure and profit level regulation.[81] With certain exceptions, the Act covers gas distribution (i.e., excluding pipelines) and electric utilities.[82] Through simplification of complex holding company structures, the Act seeks to promote and protect the integrity of public securities and to support the effectiveness of state regulation by deterring the imposition of excessive costs on operating utilities.[83]

Central to the regulatory scheme is the § 11 requirement that all non-exempt registered utility holding companies be limited in operations to those of "a single integrated public utility system" and "to such other businesses as are reasonably incidental, or economically necessary or appropriate to the operations of such integrated public utility system."[84] The Securities and Exchange Commission ("SEC") has construed the "other business" standard as limiting such non-utility activities to those which are "functionally related." With judicial approval this test has been applied restrictively to foreclose any significant diversification into non-utility related markets.[85]

Another § 11 exception allows ownership by a registered holding company of more than one integrated system where independent operations would cause a loss of "substantial economies".[86] Although not related to diversification into unregulated markets, this exception provides an important general policy litmus on allowable exceptions to the basic objectives of the Act. In *SEC v. New England Electric System*[87] the U.S. Supreme Court affirmed the SEC's position that the phrase required a loss "...so important as to cause a serious impairment" of a system's operating capability. The Court sustained the SEC's conclusion that a purported $1 million annual savings could not justify a departure from the central goal of corporate simplification.

The authority of state regulation over gas and electric utility diversification and enterprise structure has been preserved through the further exemptions of § 3(a)(1) and (2).[88] These paragraphs allow the SEC "by rules and regulations" to exempt (i) non-utility holding companies with utility subsidiaries which "are predominantly intrastate in character" and all of which operate substantially in a single state in which the holding company and every subsidiary is organized and (ii) a public utility which is itself a holding company whose operations are limited to its state of incorporation and contiguous states.

While the statute generally mandates the SEC to exempt such utilities from the Act, the SEC may deny or revoke an exemption where "...it finds the exemption detrimental to the public interest or the interest of investors *or consumers*." (Emphasis added.) In denying exemptions under this § 3 standard, or in revoking them due to changed circumstances, the SEC does not formally apply the more stringent § 11 exceptions for registered holding companies. In particular it does not automatically apply the "functionally related" test as a basis for revoking the § 3 exemption. Thus, the acquisition of water properties as part of a broader utility acquisition, although recognized by the Commissioners as not permissible under § 11, did not bar continuance of the § 3 exemption.[89] Nevertheless, the SEC's treatment of non-utility diversification in connection with exemptions has generated policy tensions.

In 1971 the Division of Corporate Regulation publicly expressed the following views on diversification trends by exempt holding companies: [90]

> When a public utility indulges in outside ventures, unrelated to its utility business, the investment caliber of its securities may decline, the costs of raising additional capital rise, and the rates charged to consumers, which support the securities, may become higher than might otherwise be necessary.

In 1973 the Commission itself addressed the issue of continuing or revoking the exemption of *Pacific Lighting Corp.* in the wake of its extensive diversification into non-utility markets.[91] As of the close of 1970 the company in recent years had invested some $82 million in six separate real estate and agricultural businesses. The four participating Commissioners were unanimous in rejecting the staff's position that the § 3 intrastate exemption incorporates the substantive standards of the § 11 exceptions. In their ultimate ruling, however, the Commissioners were evenly split. Absent a majority to revoke the exemption, the *status quo* was maintained.

Nevertheless, the "prevailing" two Commissioners declared themselves "...fully cognizant of the adverse consequences which may flow from diversification...." They considered the Commission to be charged with the duty under § 3 of "...not permitting the creation of a situation where undue risks to investors and consumers or the potential of abuse are presented as a result of expansion into non-utility activities."[92] Accordingly, their acceptance of the diversification program was conditioned on (i) the operation of non-utility activities through separate corporate subsidiaries; (ii) the prohibition of affiliate transactions except as subject to state regulatory supervision; (iii) a ban on the use of utility operating management, funds or credit for non-utility purposes and (iv) the limitation of non-utility activities to "...a relatively small component of the entire system." Adherence to these conditions would be a factor in the Commission's continuing review of the exemption status.

SEC policy on the degree of allowable diversification varies among successive Commissions as well as among contemporaneous members. In 1982 and 1983 Congressional hearings dealt with various PUHCA amendatory proposals.[93] These ranged from outright repeal (supported unanimously by the Commission) to various degrees of greater permissiveness in diversification under both § 3 and § 11.[94] No changes pertinent to the present subject were made. Accordingly, the SEC retains substantial authority to control the pace and character of non-utility diversification by intrastate utilities also subject to state jurisdiction.

As with Judge Greene's views, assessing the effect of the advent of price level regulation on SEC policy involves uncertainties which are difficult to resolve. Presumably there would be less concern about the direct impact of interaffiliate transfer pricing on costs and prices in the regulated market. But statutory concerns over capital costs and the impact of added risk on the value of securities would remain. These involve both current costs and prices of utility services and issues of longer term viability and financial integrity.

Nor have the states shrunk from the exercise of jurisdiction over intrastate public utility holding companies arguably reserved to them by the § 3 exemptions of the PUHCA.[95] It was not until 1984, however, that an authoritative federal court ruling confirmed the existence of that jurisdiction. In *Baltimore Gas and Electric Co., et al v. Heintz, et al* [96] the issue involved the validity of a Maryland statute which required prior Commission approval for the acquisition by any corporation of more than 10 per cent of the total capital stock of any Maryland public utility. [97] In a case of apparent first impression, the 4th Circuit upheld the requirement against the contention that § 3 of the PUHCA and the supremacy clause of the U.S. Constitution operated to preempt state authority over intrastate holding companies. In weighing the state's interest in the subject matter, the Court noted that the provision in issue was directed against the "particularly abusive practice" whereby holding companies "...routinely owned or operated subsidiaries in speculative non-utility enterprises...."[98]

In the year preceding this affirmation of state authority, the Massachusetts Department of Public Utilities had exercised its discretion under a similar statute to deny Boston Edison's request to restructure as a subsidiary of a Massachusetts business trust.[99] Applicant's stated purpose was to create "...a vehicle for the future entry of the company's shareholders into diversified business activities." The Department's stated standard of judgment was whether "...upon consideration of all its significant aspects viewed as a whole, the public interest is at least as well served by approval...as by...denial."[100] The Department noted the absence of any specific diversification plans and the failure of the company to propose "protective conditions or mechanisms" in response to increased ratepayer risks cited by protesting parties.

While the Department considered the *Boston Edison* record inadequate for a favorable public interest finding, it adopted no *formal* policy to bar future holding company formation by Massachusetts utilities. It did, however, intimate a preference for public utility diversification through subsidiaries. The Commission observed that such arrangements "...present more tractable review questions because the risks to the public that are implicated are bounded by the structure in which such risks occur."[101]

In New York this Massachusetts "intimation" is an established policy that permits utility diversification only through the use of subsidiaries in non-utility markets. This policy has developed in particular around the efforts of Rochester Telephone to reorganize as a holding company subsidiary. The Company's plan was first rejected in 1978.[102] The basis was in the Commission's following expressed desire for more direct control over Rochester's choice of, and investments in, new markets:[103]

> ...Rochester's acquistion of diversified subsidiaries should require our approval. Petitioners' unregulated hegemony over all potential avenues of diversification would profoundly impair our ability to regulate Rochester in the manner prescribed...because the cost of capital, insofar as it is influenced by corporate decisions about diversification, would become wholly the product of managerial discretion.... If diversification would serve rather than jeopardize Rochester's interests, Rochester can seek authorization to diversify as an independent, regulated company *instead of as a subsidiary of an unregulated company.* (Emphasis added.)

A practical consequence of this alternative arrangement arose in connection with an intended transfer of assets among Rochester's subsidiaries.[104] In 1979 the Commission authorized Rochester to invest in Rotelcom, a non-utility subsidiary, $2.2 million of revenues "...received from the rendition of utility service." A separate and more explicit provision of the order expressly required Commission approval for *any* investment above $2.2 million. Rochester in fact invested $5.4 million, of which the balance over $2.2 million was derived from dividends paid by two other subsidiaries rather than from its own utility revenues. The Commission then cited Rochester for violation of its order and sought judicial sanction for the restoration of the excess investment to Rochester.

Rochester's defense was that dividends from subsidiaries did not qualify as revenues from utility service (to which the $2.2 million limit at least arguably applied). This position was potentially complicated by the fact that the dividend paying subsidiaries were local exchange telephone companies whose dividend payments were mainly derived from revenues received in rendering utility services. In sustaining the Commission's position, however, the court ignored this legal nuance and based its decision on the explicit requirement of approval for any investment over $2.2 million.

Under an unregulated holding company structure it would ordinarily be possible to effect interaffiliate transfers among unregulated subsidiaries relatively free from regulatory authority. *The Rochester Telephone* case is indicative of the greater constraints imposed on interaffiliate asset transfers among the subsidiaries of a public utility holding company.

In 1986 Rochester again sought authority to reorganize as a holding company subsidiary.[105] In rejecting the proposal, the Commission did approve a stipulation under which Rochester could invest up to 25% of its "total consolidated capitalization, including short term debt, at any given time, in entities other than regulated utilities that provide competitive telecommunications-related goods and services." Investments in currently regulated utility assets which become deregulated are not covered in the limit. Also excluded are investments of up to 6% of total consolidated capitalization in regulated telephone utilities outside the State of New York.

In return for being ridded of the need for prior Commission approval of diversification investments within these limits, Rochester accepted the following conditions: (i) a consolidated debt ratio restriction of 40% on total capitalization; (ii) "prudent and reasonable" dividend payout and financial policies intended "... to maintain the financial integrity of its regulated telephone operations and ensure the provision of safe and adequate service at reasonable rates"; (iii) a limitation on security issuances for diversification purposes, together with prohibitions against charging the capital costs of such issuances against Rochester's operating expenses or income and against Rochester's use of regulated assets to support the financing of diversification activities; (iv) the conduct of all operations "consistent with state law; so that no subsidization by the utility operations of nonutility corporations shall take place",[106] the conduct of interaffiliate transactions "at arm's length" and the allocation of common expenses on a "fair and reasonable basis" in accordance with applicable accounting standards and requirements and (v) the provision of information and reports bearing on Rochester's investments in, and relationships with, its diversification activities.

These conditions are directed more toward protecting Rochester's general financial integrity than to detailed cost and revenue allocations. The latter issue was raised, however, by various parties who had excepted to the stipulation for its failure to include "...provision for royalty payments from the subsidiaries to compensate the utility for tangible and intangible benefits provided to them." Included among the claimed intangible benefits were "the utility's name and reputation, corporate personnel policy, corporate financing and dividend policy, and the subsidiary's access to the captive parent utility market."[107]

The Commission rejected the imposition of a royalty payment condition as a further "*quid pro quo*" for approval of the stipulation. It noted, however, that the royalty issue had been "thoroughly explored" in a separate proceeding. The Commission's ultimate position on the use of royalties for rate purposes would be based on the record in that case.[108]

By this time the separate proceeding was already the subject of an administrative law judge's recommendation.[109] That decision dealt with a specific proposal of the Department of Public Service that Rochester's principal unregulated subsidiary, Rotelcom, pay annually to the utility parent "...the greater of either 25% of Rotelcom's profits on sales to non-affiliates or 1% of its gross revenues on such sales." The ALJ found it "clear" that "...some level of royalty (or license fee) is theoretically proper." What he found more elusive, however, was an adequate basis for determining the "...proper level of the royalty that should be imputed to RTC." Accordingly, he recommended that Rochester's rates be made temporary until "...subsequently adjusted for the finally determined royalty."

These recommendations were not predicated on any identified added costs imposed on Rochester and its ratepayers through diversification. Instead (as in the separate diversification proceeding) the asserted basis for imputing revenues was in the value purportedly derived by the subsidiaries from Rochester's parentage. The Commission has not yet acted on the ALJ recommendations. A subsequent rate decision to which they might have applied involved Commission approval of a rate stipulation and moratorium in which the royalty issue was not raised.[110]

Whether the asserted rationale for royalties is based on costs incurred or values conferred by the public utility, the result is to create asymmetries of cost and value in the regulated markets. Where the amount of the royalty varies with revenues (or profits) in the unregulated markets, the revenue contribution to the regulated market is totally unrelated to its output costs. To illustrate the problem, assume that in a given year utility output costs rise by 3%, or $30 million. Assume further that the royalty rate is 10% and that in the same year the royalty revenue base rises from $300 to $600 million, resulting in a $30 million royalty increase. In the circumstances, utility output costs have increased, but prices remain unchanged. The wrong price signals are sent and demand is unduly stimulated.

Conversely, if utility output costs and royalties were to decrease respectively by $10 and $20 million, utility prices would increase in the wake of lower utility costs. In short, there is no sensible rationale for tying prices for utility service to the financial results of unregulated subsidiaries or affiliates through royalty payments.

The temptation under profit level regulation to levy a royalty "tribute" for the privilege of diversification may nevertheless at times prove irresistible. Contrary to New York Commission policy, the California Commission permits reorganization of a utility for diversification purposes under an unregulated holding company. The application of San Diego Gas & Electric for such authority led to a seminal 1986 California decision that called for royalties.[111] The Commission's approval was made subject to twenty conditions akin to those imposed by the New York Commission in *Rochester Telephone*.

As for cost allocations, Condition 3 simply required "...accounting and other procedures and controls related to cost allocations and transfer pricing to ensure and facilitate full review by the Commission and to protect against cross-subsidization of nonutility activities by SDG&E." As for transfer pricing, Condition 6(e) required at the next general rate case an independent audit of all transactions between the utility and affiliated enterprises. Interim oversight was provided under Condition 8, which required 30 day notice of any contemplated transfer from the utility to any affiliate of "any asset or property exceeding fair market value of $100,000."

In addition, however, an objecting consumer group had proposed a royalty payment "...intended to capture intangible benefits that SDO and its subsidiaries receive through their association with SDG&E." The Commission chose the label of "affiliate payments" to distinguish its proposal from the more customary usage of royalties as payments for actual value received from the use or enjoyment of patents, leases or other legal rights. The "value provided" rationale was similar to that used by the New York ALJ,[112] but emphasis was also placed on unidentified costs. The broadly asserted need was to compensate utility consumers for "...benefits, costs, and unidentified cross subsidies...by way of a payment [from the holding company and other affiliates] which will be recognized in SDG&E's utility rates."

Faced with the burden of quantifying these nebulous items, the Commission in Condition 18 required the applicants to appear as respondents in an investigation to establish "...benchmark payments, consistent with the reimbursement of expenses to ratepayers, intercompany transactions, and cross-subsidy estimates...." Moreover, the respondents' cooperation was to include a presentation of their own "best estimates" of an appropriate benchmark. In essence, Condition 18 carries no less a potential for resource misallocation than the New York proposal. The condition was a factor in San Diego's decision not to exercise its authority to reorganize as a holding company subsidiary.[113]

In 1988 the Commission (following a change of two members) considered a similar application for holding company authority from Southern California Edison.[114] Its grant of the request was made contingent on the company's acceptance of fifteen basic conditions that were mainly negotiated modifications of the *San Diego* conditions. A major addition, however, was the incorporation by reference into the conditions of "Southern California Edison Holding Company Corporate Policies and Guidelines for Affiliated Transactions."[115]

The document calls for a degree of structural separation including separate administrative staffs and, where feasible, the maintenance by "nonutility subsidiary companies" of their own facilities and equipment. Each such subsidiary, "to the extent practical", is also to provide, for its own banking, credit and insurance needs. A detailed three step cost allocation formula is applied to shared corporate functions "...such as shareholder services, corporate accounting...and planning and budgeting."

The agreed transfer pricing standard is a variant of the previously noted FCC formula. All intermarket transfers are to be at fair market value, except where net book value exceeds fair market value on assets transferred from the utility to other affiliates. In such cases, the transfer is recorded at the higher net book value. Income tax expense is to be computed by the "stand alone" method, in accordance with the Commission's "established policy."

In this case, however, royalty payments were limited to such customary uses as payment for actual transfers from the utility to the holding company of any "...product rights, patents, copyrights, or similar legal rights...." In contrast, consumer advocates had proposed that "...Edison's rates should be set as if Edison had received above-the-line income from its nonutility affiliates equal to 5% of the affiliates' gross income." The Commission rejected the proposal for failure of its proponents to show that this amount "...bears a relationship to any costs or benefits from the affiliates' association with the utility." In view of the "comprehensive transfer pricing policies" to which the utility would be subject, the Commission further concluded "...there should be no uncompensated costs incurred by utility ratepayers as a result of Edison's diversification efforts."

The dissenting Commissioner termed this decision a surrender of the Commission's "...most fundamental responsibility *to capture for all ratepayers the economies of scope and scale that are embodied in maintaining a reliable, vertically-integrated electricity network.*" (Emphasis added.) However, he would not have impressed the proposed 5% royalty on the income of all non-utility affiliates. Instead, he urged an effort to identify those non-utility affiliates whose operation would "...create a substantial probability of cross subsidies [by virtue of common costs and substantial intercorporate asset transfers]."

For the moment the matter of royalty payments from non-utility affiliates is as quiescent in California as in New York. But under continuing profit level regulation its revival may only await a more nurturing political climate.

In many states the reorganization of public utilities as subsidiaries of unregulated holding companies is regulated through the administrative implementation of governing statutes. The State of Wisconsin provides a more detailed statutory framework than most. Included among the regulatory procedures, standards and conditions (sometimes cast as "prohibitions" on the "unregulated" parent) are the following[116]:

(i)   Commission authority to "limit or cease" dividend payments from the utility subsidiary to the holding company where the utility's capital may be impaired;

(ii) prohibition on loans or guarantees from the public utility to the holding company or nonutility affiliates (although, literally, *guarantees* of *holding company debt* are not barred);

(iii) prohibition on "material" subsidies *in either direction* between the utility and nonutility subsidiaries;

(iv) prohibition on any holding company conduct that impairs the utility's ability to acquire capital on reasonable terms or to provide adequate service;

(v) prohibition of information transfers from the utility to nonutility affiliates, absent Commission approval based on availability of the information to the public on reasonable terms and the absence of any anticompetitive conduct in violation of "state or federal antitrust law";

(vi) prohibition on transfers, sales or leases of real property from the utility to nonutility affiliates "...except by public sale or offering to the highest qualified bidder" (with an exception provided for office space leases at no less than fair market value);

(vii) prohibition on combined advertising by utility and nonutility affiliates "...except for purposes of corporate identification and noncompetitive purposes";

(viii) formulaic limits on the percentage relationships between utility and nonutility assets, subject to the basic limitation for electric utilities that nonutility assets not exceed 25% of utility assets;

(ix) restrictions on the sale, installation and servicing by nonutility affiliates of appliances using the utility's primary energy source so as to encourage the use of qualified "independent contractors" for the "...installation, maintenance or service of the appliance";

(x) prohibitions of sales within Wisconsin at wholesale by nonutility affiliates of a utility of any appliance "...unless the nonutility affiliate is engaged in the production, manufacture, fabrication or assembly of any component part of the appliance" (with exceptions for swimming pools and "spa" heaters);[117] and

(xi) prohibitions on the use of utility employes in the service of nonutility affiliates "...except by contract or arrangement" approved by the Commission, subject to the conditions that the utility be compensated "...at the fair market value of the employe's service" and the absence of "unjust discrimination" against or "anticompetitive impact" on any competitor of the nonutility affiliate.

The starker political components of this statute in support of local industries would not be much affected by the replacement of profit level by price level regulation. Nor, as has been noted, would other provisions relating mainly to issues of overall financial integrity. What might be relaxed is the administrative implementation of the paragraph (iii) ban on "material" cross subsidization. Under current profit level regulation the Wisconsin Public Service Commission maintains a wary oversight of common cost allocations between the holding company and its utility subsidiary.[118]

6. Summary: Profit Level Regulation and Diversification

In the case of diversified public utility enterprises, the advent of price level regulation would not eliminate regulatory concern for the financial capability and integrity of the natural monopoly services. What could potentially be reduced or eliminated are the cost and price distortions associated with cost based rate making. Such distortions have two pervasive and persistent sources. The first lies in the absence of economically justifiable and administratively feasible non-market based cost allocation standards. The second lies in the inherent gamesmanship of the regulatory process. This results from (i) the incentives of diversified utility managers to maximize cost transfers to their regulated markets and (ii) the determination of regulators to minimize such transfers, often beyond the point of mere neutralization.

Regulated prices too often reflect the fortuitous outcomes of these dedicated counter efforts to manipulate intermarket cost and revenue transfers. The likelihood of market oriented distributions of joint and common costs in the circumstances is remote. A major potential benefit of price level regulation is the removal of these countervailing incentives.

2

The Welfare Ingredients of Price Level Regulation: Incentives and Decisional Options

A. THE FIRM'S INCENTIVES AND THEIR WELFARE IMPLICATIONS

A shift from profit to price level regulation effects a shift of risks and benefits between the firm and its consumers. In purest theory profit level regulation assigns to consumers the risks of cost increases and the benefits of cost reductions, while price level regulation reassigns both to the firm. In turn, the transfer of these risks and benefits effects a major change in the firm's incentives.

The central economic goal of profit level regulation is to replicate the theoretical results of competition by equating the firm's total costs and revenues. To the extent this goal is realized the regulated firm is largely indifferent to cost increases and lacks incentive to strive for cost efficiency. Incentives arise only from the failure of profit level regulation to meet its central goal of maintaining an equality of costs and revenues.

One principal source of such failure (in addition to the inherent complexities of cost determination) lies in regulatory lag, the delayed adjustment of revenues to cost changes. This common phenomenon is a product of transactional costs, procedural barriers and political constraints. A predictable delay in the equating of costs and revenues may induce the firm to seek an interim spread between them. This incentive is limited, however, by the prospect that the benefits of lower costs will simply be captured by consumers in the next rate proceeding. In essence, this blandishment to reduce costs is mainly an ironic and ephemeral product of a major operational defect in profit level regulation.[119]

Under conditions of regulatory lag cost efficiency may also be *compelled* by a need to avoid interim inflation based losses. The usual pressure of inflation toward cost efficiency is strengthened under regulatory lag by the firm's inability to effect more timely price increases. Neither the inducement to increase earnings nor the compulsion to maintain earnings arising from regulatory lag offers a continuing incentive to cost efficiency.

By breaking the equation between the firm's actual internal costs and allowed revenues, price level regulation regenerates the entire range of managerial incentives for profit maximization—subject to the constraint of maximum price levels. What are the likely welfare consequences of the firm's efforts to achieve the widest possible spread between costs and revenues? The question applies both to firms operating solely in regulated markets and diversified firms operating as well in unregulated markets.

The simplest answer is found in the case of the non-diversified firm serving a single regulated market. Once the maximum price level constraint (or "ceiling") is set, the firm loses control over principal (but not necessarily all) revenue enhancing efforts. Profit maximization becomes mainly a matter of cost minimization. In this vital respect the goals of productive efficiency, profit maximization and social welfare can all be well served.

Even in the single market context, however, possible conflicts between varying perceptions of overall social welfare may introduce certain complexities. The first arises from the general use of multipart rate structures throughout the scope of public utility ratemaking. These include at least a demand (or "access") charge and a commodity (or "volumetric" or "usage") charge.[120] To the extent that particular combinations of the demand and commodity component (or additional components of a multi-part rate) are perceived by the firm to increase total revenues over output costs, its interests may vary from those of regulators and some consumers. (Such differences may typically relate to the amount of the demand charge and its impact on "universal" service coverage.) The use of peak period rates provides another profit maximizing variable as to which the firm and its consumers may differ on issues of efficiency and equity.[121]

Service quality and service coverage (as the latter affects total output) may present more substantial conflicts. As to service quality, the firm under price level regulation will be more sensitive to service based demand factors. Its incentive will be to identify and maintain that level of service quality which maximizes the spread between resulting costs and revenues. Should this "optimal" level be so low as to generate public resistance, an offsetting incentive will arise to maintain higher standards sufficient to reduce complaints to acceptable levels.

Similar considerations apply to service coverage. Once output reaches the point at which marginal costs exceed marginal revenues, the firm under price level regulation (like an unregulated monopolist) will normally have an incentive to resist further expansion.[122] Further expansion in this range would only reduce the firm's profit. Under profit level regulation the marginal deficit from further expansion to meet social coverage goals will be met by rate increases.[123] Under price level regulation the firm becomes the source of any necessary "subsidy" unless the price adjustment process is sufficiently flexible to reach the same result through increases in the ceiling.

More frequently, of course, a public utility limited to the regulated sector will in fact operate in two or more distinctive markets (or service categories) within a given geographical market (e.g., residential, commercial or industrial). Under price level regulation, if each separate market is subject to a separate ceiling, the firm's incentives in each market will be the same as those of a single core market firm. Where the separate markets are combined under a single ceiling, however, the pricing incentives will change. The added aim of the firm will be to utilize elasticity differences in the separate markets to maximize the spread between total revenues and resulting output costs.

The theory can best be illustrated by the simple case of two core markets (Markets A and B) subject to a single overall constraint. Assume that while demand in each market is deemed sufficiently inelastic to warrant regulation, the degree of inelasticity in each market varies. The firm will favor a single aggregate pricing constraint that allows it to choose among a set of prices in the two markets, rather than being required to adjust each independently of the other. This will permit differential price adjustments responsive to any differential demand conditions (whether present initially or over time). In order to maintain an average price level that complies with the aggregate constraint, however, it is necessary to assign a weight to each rate category. The weighting factors might consist of relative revenues, output or costs (as identified) in the separate markets.[124]

Assume next that Market B's demand is (or becomes) less inelastic than Market A's and that Market A carries a 3/4 weight and Market B a 1/4 weight. Assume also that the initial rate per relevant output unit in each market is $10 and that output in Market A has been 3 million units and in Market B, 1 million units (thus giving rise to the initial weighting ratios, which are here assumed to govern all adjustments during a given period). On an assumption of total price inelasticity in this price range, a 10% price increase in Market A is projected to generate a 10% revenue increase (i.e. from $30 to $33 million). To offset this increase under the single ceiling constraint, the unit price level in less inelastic Market B must be reduced by $3, or 30%. Because of greater demand elasticity, however, revenues in Market B will decrease by a smaller percentage. Since the resulting revenue percentage decrease in Market B is less than the 30% price decrease, the firm will increase total revenues from the related adjustments in both markets.[125] The price changes will be profitable unless the incremental cost of the additional output in Market B exceeds the net revenue gain in the combined markets (less the incremental cost savings from any possible output reduction in Market A, should it not prove totally inelastic). In any case, the firm will prefer to be able to make the choice.[126]

With Markets A and B under a single overall price constraint the firm would be able to choose from among a large number of possible increase/decrease combinations. The choice might ordinarily be expected to reflect the "inverse elasticity rule" of Ramsey pricing theory. However, the weighting factor under a single aggregate price constraint can also force departures from Ramsey optimality.

In essence, the Ramsey pricing rule indicates that in a market of relatively elastic demand, the percentage by which price deviates from marginal cost should be lower than in a market of inelastic demand.[127] In the example given, it is suggested that a 30% price reduction in Market B will in fact generate sufficient demand to result in an overall net revenue gain. It is also possible, however, that a 30% reduction would be excessive in that a 10 or 15% reduction would generate higher net revenues than the full 30%. This fact may cause the firm to forgo the full 10% increase in Market A in order to avoid the need of a full 30% decrease in Market B. The firm's alternative would be to accept the less advantageous 30% decrease in Market B in order to obtain a greater advantage from the 10% increase in Market A. The point is that the "arbitrary" weighting factor, whether based on relative revenues, output or costs (as identified) may preclude the use of profit maximizing price adjustments within the single pricing constraint for the two markets. Indeed, in the example given, the firm may profit by lowering the price in Market B a full 30%, even if that level should fall below marginal cost.[128]

The form of any weighted price index must therefore be carefully chosen to avoid the potential for significant economic inefficiencies. The properties of such indices have not been widely considered in economics literature. One proposal that has attracted recent attention, however, is an index for a hybrid regulatory arrangement utilizing the basic element of price level regulation. Rather than an inflation less productivity adjustment formula as the constraint on maximum prices, the proposal would continue a cost based constraint. The index would weight the price for each service in each time period by the quantity produced in the previous time period. The weighted sum of prices under the index in any period would be limited to the total expenditures of the firm in the previous time period. Historical data on the firm's output level and expenditures would thus be used to constrain the profits of the firm over time. The *primary* efficiency objective of the arrangement would be the creation of conditions for long run Ramsey optimal prices rather than (as under price level regulation) the unlinking of the revenue allowance from the firm's actual costs. Thus, the immediate (but not sole) focus is on allocative rather than productive efficiency.[129]

To increase its flexibility in responding to changing and differential demand conditions, the firm will ordinarily be motivated to put as broad a range of markets as possible under a single price constraint. This aim will presumably be opposed by two groups: (i) consumers in the most inelastic markets and (ii) existing or potential competitors in markets with a measure of existing or emergent competition. In the latter case, of course, the question is whether the markets are ripe for deregulation.

The regulated firm, however, may have an incentive to retain a "quasi-competitive" market in the regulated sector. This could occur where competition requires a lower rate, whether the market is regulated or unregulated. Under an aggregate regulated price ceiling, a competitively compelled price reduction (or, as previously noted, even a price below marginal cost) could serve to justify an otherwise inadmissible price increase in the inelastic market. This would not be possible where the competitive market was either under a separate ceiling or deregulated.

An important factor affecting the firm's incentives under price level regulation will be the level of the price ceilings. Price levels erroneously set too low will encourage plant and output contraction and eventual withdrawal from the market. The ultimate constitutional right to do so will be slowed only by interim procedural constraints. Where price levels are just sufficient to maintain the firm's viability, the firm may be especially reluctant to undertake new investment. Particularly with respect to investments in innovative technology with less certain payoffs, the firm may be loath to risk incurring "failed" costs. Under profit level regulation the failure of particular increments of research and development costs to meet a test of actual productivity does not necessarily preclude their recovery as "prudent" expenses.[130] Under price level regulation the firm assumes the total risk of non-recovery.[131]

A public utility firm under price level regulation will share the usual incentives of other enterprises to enter diverse markets. These may include the availability of (i) operational economies of scope; (ii) reduced capital costs resulting from beneficial revenue and risk diversification and (iii) value creating service improvements resulting from more efficient intermarket coordination.

The diversified public utility firm operating in unregulated markets under price level regulation will experience important incentive changes from those under profit level regulation. These will flow from the firm's inability to influence its prices in regulated markets through cost increases. *To the extent that a price level regime ceases to evaluate price levels by cost based standards, the firm has no incentive to transfer costs from unregulated to regulated markets for the purpose of supporting price increases.* It might retain a related but separate incentive to record lower costs in competitive markets as a defense against claims of predation. It will, however, lose any absolution possibly resulting from improvident regulatory approval of manipulated cost allocations or transfer prices. Conversely, it will avoid the burden of defending against claims of predation based on excessive recorded costs in the competitive market, as calculated through arbitrary FDC formulas.[132]

Finally, under price level regulation the diversified firm will be ridded of a possible incentive to maintain inefficient output levels in unregulated markets. Allocative efficiency in competitive markets calls for production to the point that marginal cost equals price. Where FDC formulas distribute joint and common costs by relative output units, or relative value of output, the firm may at some point find it more profitable to restrict production in unregulated markets in order to benefit from greater cost allocations to the regulated inelastic market. Under price level regulation, the incentive is eliminated.

The impact of these incentives on the structure and efficacy of a price level regime will be considered in the remainder of this Chapter

2. What must be emphasized, however, is that these incentives (whether for better or worse) are dependent on the effective unlinking of the firm's internal costs and prices in regulated markets. To the extent that its internal costs are, or may be, reimposed as a constraint on prices, the firm will be compelled to act as if it were presently, imminently, or at least potentially, under that constraint. Most directly affected would be the firm's incentives for productive efficiency.

B. MAJOR DECISIONAL ISSUES IN A PRICE LEVEL REGIME

1. Defining the Market Scope of a Price Level Regime

Price level regulation is often characterized as a form of deregulation. NTIA described its price level recommendation as a "less intrusive government system." It drew support for its proposal from the general proposition that "Deregulation constitutes one of the great American economic success stories of the 1980's."[133]

In his abortive 1987 administrative price level proposal for the telecommunications industry in that state, Oregon's Public Utility Commissioner declared that it was made "...with the thought that the telecommunications industry in Oregon can flourish if government officials can resist the desire to fix problems that the free market can more appropriately address."[134]

In keeping with this general ethos, a common feature of price level regulation proposals has been the proposed concurrent deregulation of competitive markets. A model for such market delineation is found in the 1976 and 1980 Interstate Commerce Act amendments. These eliminated the Commission's most basic long-standing authority to establish maximum reasonable rates—except for rail movements on which the carrier is found to possess "market dominance".[135]

The common aim of all such efforts is to limit monopoly regulation to monopoly markets. The first need is for agreement on the criteria for distinguishing among markets. The measurement of market power is the subject of a vast literature.[136] NTIA's price level proposal called for the exclusion from continuing regulation of a variety of telecommunications services. It offers the following summary of standards for identifying such services:[137] a. Availability of Comparable or Substitutable Services from Alternative Suppliers at Comparable Rates; b. Number and Relative Size of Alternative

Providers and c. Existence of Entry Barriers. As previously noted, however, NTIA views deregulation more as an independent source of economic gain than as a necessary concomitant of price level regulation.[138]

The previously noted Vermont and Oregon price level proposals were limited to basic local exchange telephone services.[139] In both cases, however, the governing statute provided for the separate deregulation of competitive telecommunications services without regard to the character of regulation in the monopoly market. In Vermont, as to telecommunications services in general (whether under standard profit level regulation or under a "contract"), the regulatory board is authorized to "reduce or suspend" any regulatory requirements on determining that "...a competitive market exists for the provision of any telecommunications service...."[140] In Oregon the Commissioner's price level proposal defined its market coverage (as does the Vermont statute) by express inclusion rather than exclusion. Totally apart from this administrative proposal, the Oregon statute authorized the Commissioner's exemption from regulation of "... those telecommunications services for which...price or service competition exists...."[141]

Numerous other state jurisdictions have established procedures for total deregulation or reduced regulation in competitive telecommunications markets. In Illinois, the Commerce Commission is authorized to classify all telecommunications services as competitive or noncompetitive. As to the former, carriers may submit for Commission approval tariffs which describe "a range, band, formula, or standard" within or by which rates may be changed without prior approval. In Iowa, the statutory jurisdiction of the State Utilities Board is declared inapplicable to any telephone service or facility found by the Board to be "subject to competition". Although opposed to the FCC's "price cap" proposal and price level regulation generally, the Iowa Board advised the FCC that it had used its authority to deregulate eight separate services.[142]

This special attention to market delineation in the telecommunications industry, totally independent of price level regulation, results from the singularly dynamic proliferation of telecommunications related services. The introduction of effective competition into the (putative) natural monopoly markets of other utility sectors has proceeded at a more moderate pace. The difference is largely explained by the basic homogeneity of natural gas and electric services. Nevertheless, in both of these energy sectors supplier competition (in addition to the more usual product competition) is developing in selective markets.[143]

In theory, it would seem that the deregulation of competitive markets should go forward independent of any consideration of price level regulation. The only additional issue is whether the deregulation of competitive markets presents any policy considerations uniquely related to the structuring of a price level regime.

There are at least two such considerations. The first is that the exclusion of a competitive service from price level regulation could eliminate the perceived need (that is likely to remain under profit level regulation) to allocate substantial common costs among related regulated and unregulated services.[144] Thus, the deregulation of competitive markets under a price level regime is more likely to promote efficient pricing and output decisions in those markets.

The second consideration relates to pricing in the regulated market. It has been noted that the inclusion of competitive services in a price level regime can serve as a source of pricing flexibility. If included under the same ceiling, prices in inelastic markets may be raised to the extent of "weighted" reductions in competitive markets.[145] Should ceilings in the most inelastic regulated markets unduly reflect historical subsidy practices favoring such markets, this added flexibility could prove important to the firm's viability. Conversely, if these initial ceilings are unduly high, such flexibility may exacerbate conditions that are already inefficient and unfair. (These issues are discussed further in following sections on initial price levels and the aggregation of price ceilings.)

The identification of markets suitable for deregulation concurrent with the advent of price level regulation will invite controversy. Conflicting views on the degree of present and potential competition will require resolution. Special fact finding or dispute resolution processes may prove essential. In the end, the final definition and identification of markets to be deregulated in advance of implementing a price level regime may prove infeasible. This decisional issue is but one of several which pits political reality against economic theory.[146]

2. Determining Initial Price Levels

a.   Aggregate Levels

Under profit level regulation total revenues should in theory equal total costs. Whether the existing revenue allowance accurately reflects the firm's revenue needs will depend in part on the quality of the costing methods through which the existing allowance was determined. At their best, FDC methodologies offer little assurance of economic cost determinations. These and other contentious costing issues raise the questions of whether the existing revenue allowance warrants a presumption of validity.

Where it appears that in the absence of price level regulation existing rates would continue to serve as "base" rates, the use of a rebuttable presumption of their continuing validity might seem warranted. What must be considered, however, is that existing revenue shortfalls or excesses may be more difficult to adjust in the future under price level than under profit level regulation. Accordingly, subject to the presumption, it should be open to the contending parties to establish that the revenue requirement is either too high or too low because of material flaws in past FDC or transfer pricing mechanisms or because of other patently erroneous cost calculations (perhaps involving capital costs or depreciation).

There may well be circumstances in which the need for categorical cost adjustments may be persuasively urged. The issue of depreciation could prove of special concern. As a non-cash accounting expense with substantial cost impact in large fixed plant industries, it is an inviting target for manipulation. If the actual service life of a capital item were twenty years, with a putative service life of twenty-five years imposed by the regulator for rate making purposes, the firm must confront two problems on the advent of price level regulation. First, its annual depreciation cost will be understated; second, its depreciation reserve for replacement will be deficient. [147]

In the circumstances, the imposition of maximum prices which make no allowance for any added future investment required to make up for the reserve deficiency could strain the firm's financial viability. Following the initiation of a price level regime, the firm itself could increase its annual depreciation charge to compensate for past shortfalls. This would, of course, simply shift the revenue deficiency from the time of investment to an annual increment.

The determination of excessive or inadequate annual depreciation charges and accrued reserves is further complicated by the impacts of investment credit accounting and the varying treatments of accelerated depreciation through "normalization" or "flow through" methods. [148] Whatever these complications, the issue of depreciation can impact the firm more substantially under price than under profit level regulation. In theory, at least a portion of any deferred costs of inadequate depreciation can be recovered under profit level regulation through a future regulatory allowance for increased capital costs. Under price level regulation those costs must be absorbed entirely by the firm. Not only will the firm be required to raise more capital to cover reserve shortfalls, but the costs of that additional capital will likely increase due to equity dilution and the risks of added debt. In setting initial price levels, it therefore seems essential that adequate consideration be given to plausible claims of currently insufficient (or excessive) depreciation charges or reserves.

Where strong objections are raised to the use of the existing revenue allowance (with or without adjustments), stand alone costs offer a theoretical alternative for subsidy free pricing. As noted, this is a standard for determining maximum price levels in regulated (and unregulated) markets. In some cases the determination of stand alone costs may be impractical due to the complexities and controversies attendant on their calculation. In the relevant interstate interexchange market, the FCC rejected their use largely for this stated reason.[149]

A separate problem of stand alone costs is that they provide only upper limits on subsidy free prices. In reality the firm may provide many services and may enjoy cost savings from economies of scope. If each service were priced at its stand alone cost, the firm could well realize substantial abnormal profits. Thus, as a practical matter, the regulator may feel obligated to provide some additional constraint on the use of stand alone costs as the price ceiling (such as a constraint on aggregate profitability).

Whatever costing methodology might be used, considerations of politics and equity may deter any upward price level adjustments. Both will be involved in the central issue of whether consumers (especially in "basic" markets for "essential" services) are at least as well off under price as under profit level regulation. The path to price level regulation will not be smoothed by an explanation that consumers should not in fact be as "well off" as they are under profit level regulation.

Since public acceptance of price level regulation could be seriously impaired by an accompanying increased revenue allowance, any required increases might best be accommodated in subsequent rather than initial price levels (subject to full disclosure). One possible technique was proposed in the Oregon Commissioner's ill-fated plan covering basic local exchange telephone services.[150] (These are widely viewed as below cost services supported in part by subsidies from interexchange and business services.[151]) Thus, "...in order to gradually reduce support of local exchange services from intrastate toll and other intrastate business services" his plan would have added annually "...an additional sum equal to five percent (5%) of the difference between the rate for the basic line charge at the date of election and the basic line charge cost of service [subject to a $2 per month annual limit]."[152] A similar treatment of depreciation reserve deficiencies (or excesses) through amortization over a stipulated period might also prove useful.

In determining whether to use, or adjust, the existing revenue allowance as the basis for initial price levels, the following point must be considered: current revenue/cost deviations which may be tolerable (because ultimately correctable) under profit level regulation may not be so under the adjustment mechanisms of price level regulation.

b. Price Relationships

The same initial question applies to the issue of price relationships as to the aggregate revenue allowance. To what extent should a presumption of validity be accorded to existing price relationships and what are the alternatives where particular prices are deemed too high or low?

In theory, economically efficient initial price levels for the particular services and markets placed under price level regulation should relate to their respective marginal costs in accordance with "inverse elasticity" principles.[163] For the reasons cited in regard to the aggregate revenue allowance, the initiation of price level regulation is not the most suitable occasion for undertaking to establish such price relationships. If years of regulation have not generated economically acceptable results, it is not likely that a final spasm of effort will achieve the result. The more likely result would be the submergence of price level regulation into a quagmire of dispute. A more feasible aim would be the adoption of pricing mechanisms with sufficient flexibility to permit market oriented pricing.

Until such mechanisms are able to achieve this goal, however, the theoretical limits on the acceptance of the status quo should be recognized. Subsidy free revenues should neither exceed stand alone costs nor fall below long run incremental costs ("LRIC").[154] Where the existence of either condition can be established without undue expenditure of time and tangible resources, these limits should be honored through necessary adjustments.

In the larger and most inelastic natural monopoly markets for essential services some tighter constraints might be imposed. First, it is possible that regulators have favored a class of service to the point of driving down prices toward LRIC levels. The maintenance of maximum prices in these basic markets at just above LRIC levels could imperil the firm's viability under a price level regime—especially where competitive entries into previously protected markets serving as subsidy sources drive prices down. Conversely, it is conceivable that some markets generate revenues well above LRIC (but below stand alone costs) with the effect of failing to satisfy important consumption needs. In such cases efficiency may suffer because consumers willing to pay more than marginal costs are barred from the market.

It should therefore be open to the firm, its consumers and public representatives to prove that prices for particular services are so excessive or deficient in relation to LRIC as to constitute an imminent threat to social welfare (including the firm's viability). In most cases, however, the better part of practical economic wisdom will be to avoid the transactional costs of special LRIC studies and to provide the necessary pricing mechanisms for accommodating future prices to market conditions.

3. Price Level Adjustments

a. Programmed Adjustments: Inflation and Productivity

Inflation. If initial prices under price level regulation largely reflect costs incurred under profit level regulation, the source of any efficiency gains must be found in subsequent cost and price changes and their impacts on producer and consumer surpluses. It is in the period following the initiation of a price level regime that the unlinking of the firm's revenues and its endogenous costs will create the incentives for productive efficiency.

The major trade-off in moving from profit to price level regulation can be seen as the sacrifice of the competition replicating goal of zero profits for greater overall efficiency. The present equation of revenues and costs might seem conducive to the goal of allocative efficiency. The break in that equation under price level regulation could therefore seem retrogressive. In achieving total efficiency, however, allocative efficiency is impossible in the absence of productive efficiency. Thus, if output costs were halved while prices remain unchanged, existing consumers would be no worse off, a producer's surplus would be realized and added profitable output could be achieved through marginal cost reductions.

Accordingly, in adjusting price levels the aim is not to preclude a producer's surplus through maintenance of the revenue/cost equation. It is instead to (i) protect the firm's financial viability and (ii) permit consumers to share in the firms' efficiency gains without impairing the continuing incentives on which those gains depend.

Protection of the firm's viability first requires price adjustments to reflect the impact of inflation on its costs. The problem is to identify a wholly exogenous index that will serve as a reasonable proxy for changes in the costs of actual inputs. Once again, however, the quest for precision must be accommodated to countervailing goals—in this case the goals of certainty, ease of determination and credibility. These considerations have induced proposals ranging from the national Consumer Price Index ("CPI") (or variants limited to the Urban CPI, or regional or local CPIs) to specially constructed indices predicated on detailed studies of the weighted inputs for particular industry market sectors or firms. In between are such possibilities as the Bureau of Labor Statistic's ("BLS") Producer's Price Index ("PPI") or, as tentatively chosen by the FCC, the Gross National Product-Price Index ("GNP-PI").[155] Each has its appeal and its problems.

(1). CPI: Whether national or local, or general or urban, CPI is a measure of prices faced by consumers rather than the prices of factors of production. As a measure of all consumer prices weighted for the relative importance of *consumer* purchases, the index may be only remotely related to the inputs of particular firms or industries. The contrary point is made, however, that the index is widely known and enjoys credibility. If not an accurate proxy for production costs, it could at least serve the separate informative role of directly relating changes in general price levels to those in the regulated market.

(2). PPI: As currently constructed, the PPI is general to all industries and reflects prices received by manufacturers on first sales. Interim distribution costs such as transport (if not included in the price) and general distribution costs (including markups) are not represented in the index. To the extent, however, that changes in these latter costs maintain some approximate steady historical relationship to PPI changes, this factor in itself need not preclude the use of PPI as a useful proxy for *changes* in the firm's costs.

PPI categorical indices appear to present other problems. Thus, the "finished goods" index gives only seven per cent weight to capital equipment, which ordinarily forms a much higher component of public utility purchases. The "all commodities" index includes raw materials, which may render it more useful for measuring electric and gas utility costs, but less so for telecommunications.

(3). GNP-PI: This Department of Commerce Price Index is intended to reflect price changes in all sectors of the economy. It is therefore presumptively more representative of changes in input prices (or producer costs) than CPI, which reflects only consumer sector prices. (As an example, the GNP-PI includes prices of heavy equipment.) Even while conceding its imprecision, the FCC has tentatively chosen GNP-PI as "...a broad-based index that reflects price experience in numerous relevant markets, as compared to the narrower CPI."[156] Also, because of its relative breadth, it is less affected by

sharp changes in particular components which may be largely irrelevant to the particular cost function for which it is intended to serve as
proxy. (An example is medical costs, an important CPI component.)

The FCC may have in fact chosen the most efficacious compro-
mise between exactitude and practicality. Or its choice may be so
only in the context of the telecommunications sector. Or it may have
overestimated the difficulties of calculating, and the residual doubts
surrounding, the development of a more industry specific inflation
index. Its assessment of this issue, however, underscores the futility
of trying to project a single best index for all natural monopoly sectors in which price level regulation might be tried.

The central aim of capturing the impact of inflation on the
firms's costs provides the principal guideline in the choice of an index
for any sector. As the FCC has observed, the nature of that aim requires occasional clarification. Thus, its reminder that "While our
Notice sought to identify an index that captured changes in the purchasing power of money, i.e., a general index of inflation, its purpose
in identifying such an index was to capture inflationary changes that
the carriers themselves face. *Thus, the index we seek to adopt
should capture changes in the purchasing power of money as a measure of the cost of factors of production.*" (Emphasis added.)[157]

The range of choices and the trade-offs between precision, ease
of calculation and credibility will be similar in the case of other public utility sectors to those considered in the FCC proceeding. But the
input factors for other sectors may present unique considerations.
The question is whether the filling in of this and other important
"blanks" of a price level regime are best left to regulatory imposition,
negotiation or other dispute resolution processes.[158]

Productivity. The productivity adjustment operates as a deduc-
tion from the inflation adjustment in determining the net programmed (or periodic) adjustment in the maximum price levels.[159] In
theory, the productivity adjustment constitutes the single most critical variable in determining the success or failure of a price level
regime in satisfying the goals of efficiency and equity. In practice, its
actual relative importance may depend on how well the initial price
levels and the inflation adjustment have been chosen.

If it could be assumed that (i) initial price levels accurately reflect the firm's total and relative costs in the relevant markets and
(ii) the inflation adjustment adequately tracks the firm's subsequent
cost levels, then the productivity adjustment serves as the principle
vehicle for maintaining the firm's efficiency incentive while permitting consumers to share in its efficiency gains.

There are two principal reasons for requiring a productivity offset to inflation. First, even under conditions of cost based regulation, regulated firms have experienced some productivity gains.[160] The retention of past "normal" productivity gains by the firm under price level regulation offers no added cost reduction incentives and could result in "effortless" extra profits. Second, the sharing of added productivity gains will compensate consumers for any perceived or actual added risks of an untried regulatory regime and will thereby improve political acceptability.

The problem of the productivity adjustment is in choosing a rate which sufficiently exceeds past productivity gains so as to provide consumers with a share of *added* gains while leaving a sufficient margin to reward the firm for its efforts. This choice necessarily involves a prediction of future productivity gains under a price level regime to which past productivity experience under profit level regulation has limited relevance.

Before projecting future added productivity under price level regulation, it is necessary to determine the firm's existing productivity. This in itself involves complications. To measure the productivity experience of the individual firm will likely prove impractical, for reasons of cost and inconclusiveness. The FCC rejected the task on these grounds.[161]

One alternative in determining the existing productivity rate is the use of the most suitable neutrally published productivity index. The principal sources of such indices are the BLS and the American Productivity Center ("APC"). Neither body publishes a readily available and reliable index for use by particular utility sectors. A major failing of APC indices is their use of only two factors—labor and capital.[162] BLS uses additional factors in its "Multifactor Productivity Measure for Private Business", but has not published data for particular sectors.[163] A second alternative is to derive a kind of quasi-quantitative/quasi-intuitive assessment of existing productivity from any relevant available data, whether through particular industry or firm studies (even though disputed) or analysis of historical relationships between general and industry sector CPI indices (as noted above). In essentially this manner the FCC has tentatively chosen 2.5% as "...a reasonable estimate of potential future productivity gains *if existing regulatory methods remain in place*."[164] (Emphasis added.)

However problematic the determination of existing productivity under profit level regulation, its uncertainties are dwarfed by the problem of determining future productivity under price level regulation. The FCC addressed the issue by tentatively adopting a 0.5% additive, which it labelled a "Consumer Productivity Dividend". Its unenlightening explanation was "...that establishing [it] represents the best balancing of ratepayer and carrier interests under a price cap system."[165] By coincidence the initially negotiated British Telecom productivity factor is also 3% (i.e. Retail Price Index-3). In this case, however, the firm's productivity experience under public ownership over the prior five years was accepted by the parties, with no added "consumer dividend".[166]

A further complication lies in the possible need to distinguish between firm and industry productivity. The overall industry productivity rate, if determinable, will be a composite of individual firm rates above and below that average. Presumably, firms exceeding the average rate have modernized at a faster pace than average and will be more hard pressed to meet a *projected* future industry average based on past progress. The imposition of as high a productivity adjustment rate on such firms would penalize them for past efficiency. Conversely, firms with below average rates will benefit from past failures to modernize through accumulated future productivity opportunities that exceed the projected average. In both cases the use of an average industry projection would impair the goals of efficiency and fairness.

The dual tasks of determining existing and projected productivity rates in particular public utility sectors and for individual firms will likely require that even "final" decisions be recognized as tentative decisions. The test of experience is needed. But even assuming that this experience can be confidently projected, there will remain the issue of whether productivity gains in excess of projected gains should (i) accrue to the firm as a reward for added efficiency, (ii) should accrue to consumers to avoid "excess" profits or (iii) or should again be shared in some degree that balances efficiency and fairness.

b. Non-Programmed Adjustments:
Material and Irregular Exogenous Cost Changes

However suitable a chosen inflation adjustment may be for tracking general exogenous cost impacts, it can not encompass various material external cost impacts beyond the power of the firm or industry to control. The first problem is to determine on whom the risks and benefits of such changes should fall? In the United Kingdom the government/firm negotiators of British Telecom's Licence opted for the simplicity of the "RPI-3" formula (at least within the initial five year period). No provision was made for price adjustments based on material exogenous cost changes beyond the RPI. In such case the firm assumes the total risk of negative cost impacts and retains the benefits of any favorable impacts. Conversely, consumers are relieved of direct price level adjustment risks and forgo any such benefits. There is rough justice in this arrangement and its simplicity is appealing.

But the question remains of what to do when such changes threaten viability or create politically unacceptable windfalls. The only alternative in principle is to provide special mechanisms to change the price level in response to material exogenous cost *increases* and *decreases* not adequately reflected in the established inflation adjustment.

If such course is adopted, the first problem is to identify the nature of the changes that might support upward or downward price level adjustments. Among the prime suggested candidates are (i) tax law changes; (ii) a financially significant change in a particular cost category that constitutes a much greater portion of the firm's costs than of its weight in the inflation adjustment;[167] (iii) wholly exogenous cost reducing technological innovations; (iv) officially prescribed accounting changes that require additional reserves or the funding of existing reserves, or that eliminate or reduce existing requirements; and (v) natural catastrophes (whether befalling the firm, or other firms to its benefit).

While the causation of such cost changes can ordinarily (but not necessarily) be considered exogenous, the more difficult problem is to measure their actual impact. Can the effect of corporate income tax rate changes be varied by responsive corporate strategies? Can the impact of increases in fuel charges to an electric utility be varied in some cases by changes in fuel mix or energy sources? Accounting changes that affect income statements may not affect cash flow. Should earnings alone be considered, if in fact the firm's financial viability is not impaired? Or will it be impaired in less obvious ways because of imperfect market reactions to the earnings statement? How rapidly and to what effect are interest level changes reflected in the firm's average capital costs? Are investors properly entitled to full protection against such changes? When catastrophe strikes, will the firm's *ex parte* determinations of actual cost impact prove sufficient to support an adjustment?

It is possible to appreciate the British quest for simplicity in the circumstances. In the United States, however, the advent of price level regulation will likely be marked by strong feelings of risk aversion, shared alike by firms and their consumers. If there is a solution to this risk reduction problem, it most probably lies in (i) providing an adjustment mechanism for claims of "non-programmed" material cost impacts and (ii) limiting such adjustments to provable claims, both as to exogeneity and amount. Few such adjustments, if any, should be wholly automatic. Exceptions are warranted, however, for particular categories of exogenous cost changes known to be directly and regularly reflected in the firm's actual costs. Certain fuel cost changes (such as "arm's length" increased pipeline prices to local distributors of natural gas) might qualify for automatic treatment.[168]

Apart from the rare case of an automatic adjustment, the firm or its consumers (as represented by their regulatory agent, or otherwise) should assume the initiative in submitting claims of material financial harm or windfall. These claims should be considered in an expedited fact finding process in which the issue is the actual cost impact of the exogenous triggering event. In each case the burden of establishing the impact should fall on the claimant. This type of proceeding should have no purpose other than to accommodate material exogenous cost changes not already accommodated by the inflation adjustment. What should *not* be in issue in this particular proceeding are the firm's earnings in regulated markets.

c.   Adjusting for Differential Costs and Demand Factors

Two general issues applicable to all price level adjustments warrant brief consideration. First, as an administrative matter, it might seem advisable to apply the formulaic price level adjustment "across the board" to all price ceilings. In fact, however, the cost components of the various price ceilings may differ significantly. (They may differ as well among a group of separately priced services (or "basket") included under a single ceiling.)[169] The general inflation adjustment, the productivity adjustment, or any special exogenous cost adjustments may closely track, or widely diverge from, actual cost changes for *particular* services. As a practical matter it may well be impossible to identify and allocate these impacts. Should the effort be made? Or should the firm be free to adjust particular prices to market conditions, subject to the constraint of the overall ceiling governing the weighted adjustments to the individual ceilings?

The second issue relates to the adjustment of price levels to changes in demand that affect output and output costs. One aspect of this issue involves the impact of *endogenous* changes in the firm's own prices. This issue was alluded to by the FCC in the following statement from its initial rulemaking notice: "For each adjustment triggering a change to price caps, we would also need to determine the extent to which we would take into account the stimulation or repression of demand likely to arise from the change in rates allowed as a consequence of the change to the price cap."[170] The issue is not resolved in its *Further Notice*.

The other equally important aspect of demand related price level adjustments involves the impact of exogenous demand factors. The

FCC's tentative proposal in its *Further Notice* does not raise the issue; nor does it arise in the British Telecom license. In his Second Annual Report for 1985, however, the Director General made these remarks:

> The RPI-3 rule is attractively simple. However, in telecommunications, the cost per unit of dealing with an increase in the volume of business tends to be much below the average cost for existing business. This means that a simple formula will tend to produce profits that are higher than expected and it tends to produce profits that are lower than expected in times of business recession. If some sacrifice of simplicity is acceptable, this difficulty can be avoided by including the volume of business as a specific element of the price control formula.[171]

This passage describes the normal declining cost pattern of characteristically high fixed cost natural monopoly firms. Throughout the range of output marked by declining average costs, such a firm will experience lower costs and higher net earnings per unit of output. Absent any consequential price adjustments, under price level regulation the firm itself will be the beneficiary of greater demand resulting from external economic conditions. Conversely, under conditions of general economic contraction, the firm would assume the risk of lower output and earnings. In contrast, under profit level regulation compensating rate adjustments could be imposed on, or sought by, the firm (taking into account demand elasticity in the relevant markets as a normal incidence of the rate making process).

Although the Director General's "quasi-recommendation" mainly addresses the impact of prices and general economic conditions on demand, any consequential price adjustment to reflect "volume of business" changes would apparently be implemented without distinction as to cause (which, for example, might be attributed to service quality). As yet this suggestion has not been incorporated in a license amendment. The failure of the FCC or the Director General to proceed further in considering demand related price level adjustments poses the question of whether changes in demand materially affecting the firm's costs and possible viability should or could be accommodated under a price level regime.

The science of econometrics seems capable (subject to varying degrees of credibility) of predicting the impact on demand for a firm's services of changes in its own prices or in broader economic indicators. Since demand factors, whether external or internal to the declining average cost firm, can materially affect output and output related costs, it may be prudent to incorporate demand factors into cost related price level adjustments. Should this be done?

As regards a demand related adjustment to reflect changes in the firm's own prices, the first problem is that of utilizing wholly exogenous adjustment processes. This is essential for avoiding controversies that would inevitably arise from reliance on the firm's own projections, or on "neutral" projections of others based on firm supplied data. What might be required is econometric analysis bearing on the more general impact on demand of price changes in comparable product and service markets. (The projections should presumably include the increment of price change resulting from the inclusion of the demand factor in the price adjustment formula.)

As regards the inclusion in the inflation adjustment of macroeconomic factors affecting demand and output, there are separate problems. First, of course, like the problem of the possible alternate use of CPI, PPI, GNP-PI, or an industry specific cost inflation index, the demand related index should be reasonably related to the firm's markets. Assuming such an index is available, the second problem is that of applying historical data to future prices. Indices derived from a past period may not be relevant to demand conditions in a subsequent period. The need may be for demand factor adjustments based on projections of demand conditions during the period in which the resulting price level adjustment will apply. In a climate of controversy, however, there is rarely anything automatic about projections, whether by the firm or "exogenous neutrals".

While the difficulties of incorporating demand factors (whether endogenous or exogenous) into the price adjustment formula are clear enough, the possible consequences of failing to do so can not be ignored. First, consider the effect on demand, output, costs and profits resulting from price level adjustments alone. For simplicity, the example of a single product firm can be used.

Assume that the inflation less productivity factor represents the firm's actual cost increase in the past period and warrants a five percent increase in the price ceiling. Assume further that at rates in force at the outset of the prior period the firm was earning a normal return (i.e. total revenues equal total costs). (This might occur where actual productivity has exceeded the productivity factor in prior years.) What is the impact of a five percent price increase?

If the firm experiences constant returns to scale, the five percent cost increase will raise average costs by that amount regardless of output. The five percent price increase, however, will presumably lower demand. Because returns to scale are constant the firm's total return remains normal. In this case, the firm's viability is not affected.

In the more usual case of increasing returns to scale, however, the same circumstances will impair the firm's viability. Starting again from a break-even point, the five percent price increase simply covers the five percent cost increase; but with increasing returns to scale, reduced demand and output will result in additional average cost increases above the five percent price increase since average cost increases as output declines.

Under conditions of subadditivity it is also possible for a natural monopoly to display decreasing returns to scale over some range of output.[172] In such case within that range the reverse circumstances would result in an abnormal return. As output decreases in response to the price increase, average costs will decline.

Generalizations can not be made regarding the effect on the firm's return of the failure to include price related demand factors in the price adjustment formula. The particular impact will depend on the cost structure and the nature of the demand curve in which the price adjustment occurs. Under any circumstances the concern is that a price adjustment mechanism intended to reflect changes in input cost levels only will generally omit the important considerations of scale economies and demand elasticity.

The problems are similar where shifts in demand result from exogenous factors. The point is made by considering the effect of a reduction in general income levels on a firm whose single natural monopoly market operates with increasing returns to scale. Assume that in the recessionary economy the inflation/productivity factor leaves prices unchanged. As demand and output fall in reponse to lower income levels, the average cost per unit of output increases. The firm's viability is again impaired due to its inability to raise prices to resulting cost levels.

The questions previously posed in relation to the difficulties of incorporating demand factors into the price adjustment formula now take on a reverse emphasis. Despite the problems, should the effort *not* be made? Is it really feasible to allow unadjusted demand factors to be suffered or enjoyed by the firm until the consequences become intolerable to someone? In the end, the choices are: (i) to provide for programmed demand related changes in the price adjustment formula; (ii) to permit non-programmed adjustments when the case can be made; or (iii) to provide the firm with sufficient pricing flexibility to justify its assuming the risk of responding to demand conditions. (It must be noted, however, that in the absence of external subsidies the firm's assumption of some risk is unavoidable. In the example above, even if exogenous demand conditions were factored into the price adjustment formula, the question remains of whether conditions of price elasticity would permit full recovery of the revenue shortfall. Any further effort to raise prices to compensate for lower output could be self-defeating.)

4. Price Structure and Relationships: Aggregate and Disaggregate Ceilings

In general, the firm's pricing flexibility will vary with its ability to offset increases in markets of lesser elasticity with decreases in markets of greater elasticity.[173] The firm's incentives for setting particular prices as close as possible to levels at which the spread between revenues and incremental costs is maximized has been noted.[174] Its ability to do so is largely a function of the number of separate prices available for a "basket" of services under a single ceiling. As the number of prices within the single ceiling increases, so do the opportunities for profit maximizing tradeoffs.

What is profit maximizing for the firm, however, may arouse the opposition of consumers in markets of inelastic demand and competitors in other markets. In some instances their equity based concerns may find support in efficiency concerns. Perhaps the most striking example lies in the possible incentive of the firm to price under its incremental costs—not for predatory purposes—but for the greater net revenue advantage available through its ability to raise prices in the monopoly market.[175] Clearly, the central issue in establishing price structures and relationships under a price level regulatory regime involves the classic polarities of public utility price regulation—promoting the efficiency gains of market oriented pricing while preventing exploitation of consumers in monopoly markets and predation in competitive markets.

Assuming a continuing mix of market elasticities under a price level regime, various techniques are available in striking a balance. In the case of British Telecom, as noted above, maximum flexibility derives from the coverage under a single ceiling of all regulated services subject to the RPI-3 constraint. These services include (i) the rental charge for the basic exchange line, both residential and business (i.e. the "access" charge), (ii) dialed local exchange calls and (iii) dialed interexchange calls. Assuming a 3% overall authorized increase in a given year (i.e., RPI=6), under its license authority the firm could apply an increase in excess of 3% to the most inelastic access charge, subject to any necessary weighted offset in the most elastic interexchange market. Instead, for the license term the firm (as previously noted) has undertaken to limit any annual exchange line rental increase to 2%.[176]

The limitation of price increases or decreases to a particular percent deviation from the existing base ("banding") is another means of applying constraints to a broad basket of services (or rate classifications) weighted under a single ceiling. Thus, in the preceding British Telecom example, rather than placing a percent limit on increases in the market of greatest inelasticity, a limit could be placed on decreases and increases for all services. Where demand for services in a given price category is influenced by competition as well as price alone, the banding of prices to constrain decreases (as well as increases) could serve the dual regulatory purposes of limiting the use of a decrease as an offset to other increases and of deterring "unduly" aggressive competitive reductions at or near marginal costs limits.

In seeking a suitable balance among its pricing objectives in interstate telecommunications markets, the FCC has tentatively selected a combination of "baskets" and "bands".[177] For flexibility it proposes to group all prices within only two baskets—one for all switched services, the other for all private line services. Its purposes are to include cross-elastic (or "substitutable") services within the same basket and "...to simplify administration of the allocation of adjustment factor changes."[178] The requirement of two baskets rather than one, however, is intended as a limit on flexibility by thwarting any incentive to use significant elasticity differences between these two major service groupings for "cross-subsidization".[179]

The additional banding limit on flexibility serves a similar purpose as regards elasticity differences among services within a single basket. The FCC proposes a 10% band which would thus permit "...after applying the Price Cap Index...a 5 percent fluctuation above and below existing rates."[180] A final structural variant is intended to allow increased flexibility for competitive price decreases while limiting the use of such decreases as offsets to price increases in more inelastic markets. This would be accomplished through the creation of a "no credit zone" below the 5% band. The aim is to stimulate lawful competition while deterring predation through denial of potential subsidies.[181]

The basic choices in establishing price structures and relationships under a price level regime are thus contained in the British Telecom and proposed FCC "price cap" arrangements. These choices will be common to regulated markets in all public utility sectors, but their use must be adapted to the differing characteristics and relationships of the various markets. The problems could prove less complex in the electric and natural gas industries, where service classifications mainly reflect differences in consumer usage patterns rather than in the nature of the service. Nevertheless, the major aim will be to achieve an optimal balance between pricing flexibility and the protection of consumers in the most inelastic markets.

Some guidelines will be more apparent than others. For example, the inclusion of industrial services with bypass alternatives and basic residential services under a single ceiling is clearly questionable.[182] The central purpose of any inflation less productivity formula is the protection of consumers in basic residential markets. In general, the allowance of increases above the formula in these markets (other than as an agreed arrangement to "amortize" established pre-existing subsidies) could quickly erode the credibility of price level regulation. To justify "above formula" increases in basic residential markets by competitive price reductions in industrial markets would likely prove politically intolerable. (Political intolerability, however, is no reliable measure of social utility. Where price constraints in basic residential markets have been set so low as to threaten the firm's viability, competitively compelled price reductions for industrial customers could provide an economically justifiable escape hatch.)

Even in the "homogeneous" service industries the grouping possibilities are substantial considering (in addition to industrial classifications) the various categories of residential use (e.g., basic, air conditioning, water and space heating), commercial use, special high volume use (e.g., large multiple dwelling developments with sub-metering or rent inclusion) and public uses (e.g., traction, street lighting and public buildings). Peak period pricing, whether seasonal or time of day, must also be factored into the service groupings. In addition, the access, volume usage and any other material elements of basic rate classifications may be accorded separate weighting in any grouping structure.

Accordingly, one means of reducing the level of continuing controversy, would be to deregulate the most price elastic markets subject to consumer bypass due to alternate suppliers or substitutable products or services. The remaining differences in market elasticities should provide adequate potential flexibility for adjusting regulated prices to market conditions. However, the deregulation of markets and the initiation of a price level regime may well be beyond the capacity of a single proceeding to resolve.[183] As with the other essential elements of a price level regime, the problem of establishing a price structure and price relationships might best be committed to a special dispute resolution process capable of generating an economically efficacious and politically acceptable accord.

Beyond these major substantive pricing issues, are other ancillary substantive issues and the regulatory mechanics of the pricing process. One additional substantive issue involves the treatment of new services offering an additional service option (as distinguished from the "restructuring" of an existing service option).[184] The problem is more nettlesome in the telecommunications sector where new services proliferate as the products of new technologies.[185] But the basic ingredients of the problem are present in all regulated public utility markets.

Where a new service classification option is combined with retention of existing classifications the problem of an unreasonably high price for the new service does not arise. The continuing services will provide an effective brake.[186] In theory, however, a problem of discriminatory pricing could be presented by a new service classification so constructed as to limit its use to a favored consumer or consumer class. Even where the firm's motivation lies solely in market conditions, the issue of cost/price relationships and the necessity of the particular classification may nevertheless arise. Under what circumstances should the proposed new classification and its price be suspended? What showing, if any, should be required to avoid suspension or to justify initiation following suspension? Should the incorporation of the new service into the price structure await its actual usage in order to assign a realistic weight? Or should a "constructive" weight based on demand projections be assigned *ab initio*? In what basket should it be included?

Among the issues of mechanics and process are (i) the time intervals for effecting programmed inflation less productivity price adjustments, (ii) the time periods for which the adjustments are calculated (e.g., the use of recent "spot" data versus averaged change over a longer period), (iii) procedures for determining and implementing non-programmed price adjustments, (iv) notice requirements of programmed and non-programmed price changes, (v) notice requirements for interim price level adjustments within the prescribed ceilings and possible frequency limitations on interim changes and (vi) the nature of supporting data to establish that interim price adjustments fall within applicable ceilings. The resolution of these issues requires a balance between maximum pricing flexibility in reponse to changing market conditions and the maintenance of public confidence in the integrity and stability of the pricing system.

3

Assessing the Efficacy of Price Level Regulation for the Natural Monopoly Markets of Diversified Firms[187]

A. POTENTIAL BENEFITS OF PRICE LEVEL REGULATION

1. Productive Efficiency and Innovation in Natural Monopoly Markets

In seeking to replicate the results of competition through limiting the firm's revenues to its costs, profit level regulation has only succeeded in reducing consumer welfare by increasing production costs. Efforts to tinker with costs by disallowing this or that category or increment simply pits the regulator against the firm in an unending and costly game. The most effective regulatory regime is a poor proxy for the firm's own efficiency incentives.

The central attraction of price level regulation lies in its incentives, and therefore its potential, for productive efficiency. This potential covers general cost efficiency within the firm's existing technology and for cost reducing, value creating innovation through new technologies. The amount (or, more realistically, the percentage range) of potential cost reduction is difficult to project and will vary among sectors and firms. What seems incontrovertible, however, is that the effective unlinking of the firm's revenue allowance from its own internal costs will provide a powerful new impetus to the production of required output at minimum cost.

2. Allocative Efficiency

a. Pricing in Natural Monopoly Markets

The focus of profit level regulation on the equating of total revenues and costs casts a long shadow on the pricing of particular services. Given this central regulatory objective, it is only natural that the norm for all prices tends to be the total costs of the product or service. Under profit level regulation market oriented departures from "full cost" pricing in response to differential demand conditions may be allowed where contributions to overheads from more elastic markets are increased to benefit inelastic markets. Such departures, however, constitute exceptions to the general rule and are scrutinized accordingly. Competitors claim predation and consumers in inelastic markets (often the unwitting and unwilling beneficiaries) claim favoritism to others. The issues must be tried. The firm's claims of justification based on differential demand conditions must be proved. In all, the environment of profit level regulation deters rather than encourages demand based pricing oriented toward marginal rather than full costs.

A particular irony of this process lies in the nature of the "full cost" standard from which departures are impeded under profit level regulation. "Full costs" are "fully distributed costs", derived through arbitrary allocations of joint and common costs. These costs reflect accounting calculations rather than economic assessments. Far from offering a useful norm of allocative efficiency or presumptive legality, FDC fails on both counts.

Conversely, the unlinking of total revenues and costs under price level regulation will remove the dominant model for full cost pricing in regulated markets. Constraints on demand oriented individual prices will tend to become the exception to the rule rather than the rule itself. Such constraints may continue to be imposed to deter below marginal cost pricing or to limit offsetting increases in basic service markets of highest inelasticity. In general, however, the advent of a price level regime should bring with it enhanced incentives and opportunities for greater allocative efficiency through (i) the conceptual unlinking of prices and full costs, as determined through FDC methodologies and (ii) a greater consequential emphasis on demand oriented norms.

b. Pricing and Output in Unregulated Markets

In similar manner the *effective* unlinking of total revenues and costs in regulated markets would eliminate the firm's incentives to shift costs from unregulated to regulated markets. This new condition would apply alike to incentives for manipulating FDC formulas used to allocate joint and common costs; for transferring assets *from* the regulated market at recorded prices below market value and *to* regulated markets at recorded prices above market value; and for possibly restricting output in unregulated markets in order to effect larger cost allocations to the regulated market under existing FDC formulas based on revenue or output. The elimination of the transfer cost linkage of regulated and unregulated markets should permit the latter to operate under market conditions to the same degree as firms having no ownership and control relationships to regulated natural monopoly markets.

3.   Reducing the Costs of Regulation

The following FCC statement applies generally to profit level regulation:[188]

> Cost-of-service regulation...even if done correctly and well...imposes significant costs on regulated firms and those they serve. The policies and rules we have developed to make this method of regulation work are complicated: their application and enforcement are a resource intensive activity for the regulator, the regulated firm and other interested parties.

The question is whether these direct regulatory costs could be substantially reduced under a price level regime.

It can be intuitively posited that in some important part the direct costs of regulation are a function of the degree of compatibility (or incompatibility) between regulatory objectives and the firm's incentives. The direct costs of profit level regulation arise, therefore, largely from the need to monitor and control (i) the firm's general cost levels (especially capital costs) and (ii) cost transfers between markets of greater and lesser elasticity (whether the latter are regulated or unregulated). As again stated by the FCC with regard to profit level regulation: "...this form of regulation is inherently expensive because it requires a tremendous volume of cost and earnings data, and a large number of carrier filings and reports."[189]

While price level regulation would hardly eliminate the direct costs of regulation, it has some potential for reducing those costs. The stronger the firm's cost reduction incentives and the weaker its incentive to manipulate intermarket cost transfers, the greater the likelihood of significant regulatory cost reductions. Actual realization of the potential benefits of this welfare enhancing incentive structure will depend on the extent of regulatory recourse to cost based oversight standards in measuring the firm's performance. As previously observed, where the firm anticipates an imminent need to justify its financial performance under traditional cost standards, then the incentive structure of profit level regulation will be revived. In turn, the regulatory trappings and costs of a profit level regime will again become a necessity.[190]

Even without these particular trappings and costs, price level regulation will incur costs from the need to respond to other possible "negative" incentives not necessarily compatible with legitimate regulatory objectives. Specifically, the monitoring of service quality and the firm's adherence to its service coverage obligation will be required.

Regulatory costs will also arise from the normal administration of programmed (or "automatic") price adjustments and tariff requirements. More substantial costs may flow from contested proceedings involving proposed non-programmed cost adjustments. Overall, however, assuming minimal reliance on cost based monitoring and performance standards, profit level regulation could lead to significant reductions in direct regulatory costs.

B. POTENTIAL PROBLEMS
OF PRICE LEVEL REGULATION[191]

1. Potential Pricing Problems

Under price level regulation the problems of pricing and service coverage are closely related. Thus, difficult pricing issues could arise from the firm's general inability to raise price levels in support of unprofitable, but socially desirable, output expansion.

Under profit level regulation core public utility markets constitute a vast and complex network of price discrimination. Discrimination exists not only among separate service classifications, but within any single classification. In the case of electric and gas distribution, for example, the price/cost relationship for a given consumer may be a function of the consumer's location and consumption patterns.

Given these differing factors, many consumers are served at prices that exceed the average costs of service. Many others enjoy prices below those average costs. This discrimination is justified, not by compelling demand differences, but by the avoidance of the transactional costs required to identify individual consumer costs and to administer a price structure reflecting those costs. The elimination of these added costs is thought to leave most "subsidizers" better off than they would otherwise be under a price structure that attempted to reflect individual consumer costs.

Price equalization within a broad service classification is often applied without regard to whether some prices below average incremental costs are not in fact below marginal costs. But the practice is not without limits, even under profit level regulation. The use of price equalization for a new subdivision within the city requiring an extended distribution system may be tolerable both politically and economically. The financing of costly new generating capacity to meet seasonal peak demands for air conditioning may be neither. Over the past two decades the general trend has been toward the adoption of marginal cost price structures, especially in the circumstances of decreasing returns to scale.[192]

Marginal cost pricing achieves the objective of general economic efficiency. In the case of seasonal peak demand, it serves as well the direct need for financial viability. Its principles enjoy equal validity under profit or price level regulation. The difference in its usage under the two regimes, however, relates primarily to the firm's viability. For the firm subject to *decreasing* returns to scale, price level regulation may exacerbate the need for marginal cost pricing to recapture the added costs of capacity expansion. That need would arise from an inability to finance expansion by general price increases.

Consumer resistance to marginal cost pricing may occur where the class of consumers whose demand creates the need for capacity expansion is substantially the same as the general consumer base. Recently, pursuant to a proposal to the Illinois Commerce Commission, Commonwealth Edison reduced its summer "premium" rates and, in effect, reallocated the resulting incremental revenue requirement to the normal non-seasonal service classification.[193] A major contributing factor to the proposal and its implementation was a widespread preference of air conditioning consumers to avoid "summer rate shock" by absorbing the "premium" for added costs in their year round rates.

In similiar circumstances, the firm under price level regulation whose need was for a new seasonal service classification to deal with decreasing returns to scale might expect even stronger resistance to new marginal cost based service classifications. The economic need for a higher rate classification would exist, but (other than for possible constitutional considerations) the legal entitlement for an "escape hatch" from the prevailing price level may not. Nor, in the alternative, would there be entitlement to a general price adjustment not provided for in the programmed adjustment formula or in the nonprogrammed exogenous cost adjustment mechanism. However great the need, the firm's necessary response would be to resist expansion in the absence of price increases required to meet the higher unit costs from added capacity. In short, the Averch-Johnson incentive toward over investment could be reversed with a vengeance.

The particular problem of pricing for costly capacity expansion is a more critical aspect of the broader problem previously noted—the inclusion in the pricing calculus of changes in demand and their impacts on costs. Added concern for the firm's viability renders the matter of price structure (and particularly of marginal cost oriented service classifications) of even greater importance under price level regulation. Either demand factors in the context of the firm's cost structure must be included in the price adjustment mechanism, or the firm must be allowed broad flexibility in establishing new service classifications and prices that permit the recovery of demand induced expansion costs not otherwise reflected in that mechanism.

2. Potential Problems of Service Coverage and Quality

The determination of efficient output levels and service coverage under price level regulation may create other conflicts between entreprenurial perceptions of transactional efficiency and public perceptions of social efficiency. These conflicts are ameliorated under profit level regulation by the firm's ability to obtain compensation for below cost services through general rate increases within the same service classification. This support (together with any interclassification subsidies) has provided the financial base for the social goal of "universal service". The initial ceilings under price level regulation may be sufficient to permit some continuation of this traditional support for socially desired service coverage. It may prove insufficient, however, to allow any appreciable expansion without threatening the firm's viability.

Within the limits of public tolerance, the firm will be motivated to eliminate or reduce output of all services that can be identified as failing to return incremental costs under existing price levels. Low income consumers unable to meet the basic price level can be served through public subsidies paid to the firm for revenue shortfalls, or special service classifications for qualified "low income" consumers. The latter solution would require offsetting increases in the general price ceiling. Such arrangements would be consistent with current pricing trends.[194]

For reasons of its public standing, the regulated firm on the advent of a price level regime is not likely to initiate major revisions in service coverage standards. Nevertheless, a pull toward profit maximization may create new tensions in the firm's commitment to meeting social goals for service coverage. These might be reduced through further specificity in defining the firm's "obligation to serve". Satisfaction of the obligation would be supported through the alternatives suggested in the preceding paragraph.

With regard to service quality, the basis for any concern under price level regulation (as previously noted) would arise from the firm's possible perception that some lesser amount of operating costs would produce no more than a tolerable increment of service deterioration. The incentive to reach this conclusion lies in reduced maintenance costs. But the incentive will operate only to the point that the financial and psychic costs of dealing with the complaints of consumers and regulators are less than the added profits.

Under profit level regulation the firm has every incentive to avoid these psychic costs by whatever expenditures are needed to sustain public satisfaction. Indeed, to minimize such costs the firm may err on the side of excessive expenditures in support of service quality. (This managerial desire for an "easier life" is but one aspect of the incentives to inefficiency under profit level regulation.) Even in these circumstances, however, regulators have established service standards for reliability, technical quality and responsiveness to complaints. Should the firm under price level regulation feel a lesser spur to meeting those standards, the need could arise for added fines or penalties. Service quality, however, constitutes a most sensitive and exposed element of the firm's operations. With or without continuing regulatory scrutiny, it seems unlikely that a firm not under acute financial stress will be inclined to opt for any appreciable decline in service quality.

3.   The Potential Problem of Errant Indices

The choice of an inflation adjustment index for price level regulation is not intended to create a condition of "Russian roulette" for either the firm or its consumers. What should be chosen is the closest feasible proxy for measuring cost changes in the firm's actual inputs. In itself, the inflation index should serve neither as a source of windfall profits to the firm nor windfall surpluses to consumers. The principal efficiency mechanism from which the firm, its consumers and society are intended to benefit under price level regulation is the firm's incentive to reduce costs beyond the chosen productivity factor.

These apparent truisms are of critical importance in considering the treatment to be accorded major unanticipated deviations between changes in the inflation adjustment factor and the cost levels of the firms's actual inputs. The problem has occupied the courts in recent years in regard to inflation adjustments under negotiated private sector contracts. Such decisions reveal the type of problems which will be encountered. The three such cases which follow illustrate a variety of index "aberrations", their consequences and the court's conclusions.

(i)   *Missouri Public Service Co. v. Peabody Coal Co.*[195]

The 10 year coal supply contract called for a $5.40 per ton base price, subject to an inflation escalator clause. Seller had proposed CPI, but buyer successfully negotiated use of the Industrial Commodities Index ("ICI"), based in large part on material production costs. At time of trial seller's claimed losses on the contract were $3.4 million, of which 40%, or $1.36 million was attributed to the failure of the ICI inflation escalator to reflect seller's cost increases accurately. It was not disputed that had CPI been used, "...seller's purported losses would have been substantially reduced."

The evidence supported seller's claim that in the years preceding the contract ICI had been an accurate measure of inflation, but had then ceased to be due to "... the 1973 oil embargo, runaway inflation and the enactment of new and costly mine safety regulations." Consequently, ICI lagged behind CPI in reflecting cost inflation, and particularly in relation to seller's actual costs.

In allowing buyer's request for specific performance, the state appellate court rejected seller's defense based on the Missouri doctrine of "commercial impracticability". The court observed: "That such indexes were based on different commercial and economic factors was presumably known by both parties since each was skilled and experienced in those areas and the divergence between the indexes could not be said to be unforeseeable. Be that as it may, [seller] agreed to the use of the [ICI]."[196]

(ii)   *Aluminum Co. of America v. Essex Group, Inc.*[197]

The original 16 year contract covering the conversion of "buyer's" aluminum ore into aluminum by "seller" was subject to a 5 year extension at buyer's option. The contract price for conversion provided that $.03 per pound of the original price of $.15 would escalate in accordance with the Wholesale Price Index-Industrial Commodities ("WPI-IC") published by the Bureau of Labor Standards of the Department of Labor. Other components of the $.15 also escalated or varied by other indices not pertinent here. The entire indexing system was proposed by seller and was evolved "...with the aid of the eminent economist Alan Greenspan." Notwithstanding the illustrious parentage of its own index proposal, seller sought reformation or equitable adjustment based on mutual mistake of fact arising from the failure of WPI-IC to reflect unanticipated costs in respect to a $.03 per pound base price, or one-fifth of the total original price.

Seller claimed to have sought through operation of the *total* index "...a stable net income of about 4 cents per pound of aluminum converted." Its range of "foreseeable deviation" was "roughly" $.03 per pound, or between $.01 and $.07 per pound. Initially, the index system operated as anticipated. Beginning in 1973, due to "...OPEC actions to increase oil prices and unanticipated pollution control costs...", the cost of electricity, "...the principal non-labor cost factor in aluminum conversion...", rose much more rapidly than WPI-IC. In the five year period 1968-1973, seller's actual non-labor production costs rose from $.04371 to $.05819, or 18.7%. Between 1973 and 1978, these costs rose to $.22717, or 390%. The cumulative 1968-1978 increase was 520%, as compared to a WPI-IC increase in the same period of 204%. A steady decline in total contract profits from 1972-1978 had resulted in a loss per pound in 1978 of $.10484 and a total loss on the contract of $8.62 million.[198] The court found that total losses over the term of the contract would exceed $60 million.

Seller sought to "reform or equitably adjust" the contract on the theory of mutual mistake of fact. The court agreed and found "the parties' mistake" to be "...one of fact rather than one of simple prediction of future events." The court emphasized the underlying intent of the parties to utilize "an objective pricing formula" that would yield predictable results. Thus, their mistaken assumption was "...essentially a present actuarial error." The formula adopted was intended "...to protect against vast windfall profits to one party and vast windfall losses to the other...."

The court found at stake in the case "...the future of a commercially important device—the long term contract." Should the law fail to provide an appropriate remedy "...when a prudently drafted long term contract goes badly awry, the risks attending such contracts would increase." Accordingly, the issue to be addressed is whether "...the deviation between the index and the pertinent costs of the parties was adequately foreseen and its risk allocated in the contract."

(iii) *Printing Industries Ass'n v. Graphic Arts International Union, Local No. 546.*[199]

Certain labor agreements covering employees in the Greater Cleveland area included a cost-of-living allowance ("COLA") based on the Cleveland CPI Revised for Urban Wage Earners and Clerical Workers ("CPI-W"). The "local" index had been proposed by employers and accepted by the union as a reasonable measure of inflation encountered by employees in the area. Nevertheless, employers now sought reformation of the contract through substitution of the national CPI-W. Their claim was based on an "unprecedented distortion in October 1982" resulting in a 56 cent per hour wage increase, or 36 cents per hour more than if calculated under the National CPI-W. The alleged aberration was attributed to a disproportionate weight placed on the housing component of the index and statistical distortion resulting from a smaller number of sales.

As in *Alcoa,* the court found a mutual mistake of fact. Contrary to the *Alcoa* outcome, however, the court concluded that "...the variance between the Cleveland CPI-W and the national CPI-W was a risk assumed by the parties." Accordingly, reformation was deemed inappropriate "...simply because subsequent information has revealed that an index upon which both parties relied and which had been accurate over a number of years suddenly changed." In choosing the other side of *Alcoa's* conceptual coin, the court expressed a countervailing concern that "The finality of contract and the certainty of the parties would be subject to the variability of fluctuations and 'whose ox was gored'."

The distinction among these cases, however, is more factual than conceptual. *Alcoa* might be said to stand apart in three major respects from the two cases in which the contract is enforced despite index aberrations—(i) the length of its term, (ii) the extent of the deviation from reasonable projections and expectations and (iii) the extent of the financial impact.

The issue of index aberrations will undoubtedly arise in the administration of price level regulatory arrangements. The cases described offer some direction toward the development of appropriate standards of materiality. But the possible distinctions between private and public contracts must also be considered.

Parties to long term contracts of either type are generally loath to view inflation as a gamble to be won or lost. In the case of public utility prices the level of tolerable risk will likely be lower than in the majority of commercial transactions. Both the regulated firm and its consumers must plight their troths in the same natural monopoly markets whose operations can have widespread and substantial economic effects. The political and economic consequences of serious loss to either party in the matter of public utilty prices requires special concern for the problem of index aberrations. Where major and largely unforeseeable index deviations impose unintended and serious hardships or confer substantial and unanticipated windfalls, reformation may be appropriate.

The problem, of course, is where to draw the line. Not every discernible deviation from the expected performance of an inflation index in reflecting the firm's actual costs can become the occasion for reformation proceedings. The resulting costs of resolution could prove prohibitive. Nevertheless, using the procedures for non-programmed price adjustments, it should be open to the firm or consumer representatives to raise issues of hardship or windfall resulting from "errant" indices. If need be, frivolous claims can be discouraged by cost assessments.

The principal focus in such proceedings should be on the extent of the deviation between inflation indexed costs and the actual impact of inflation on the firm's inputs. Any resulting price adjustments, or changes in the inflation index as the basis for future price adjustments, should reflect that deviation. The exception would lie in the firm's failure to undertake reasonably available endogenous measures to offset unexpected exogenous cost increases.

The firm's earnings should rarely provide the focus for such proceedings except where its financial viability is shown to be threatened. As a general rule, the fruits of the firm's own successful efforts to improve its productivity should not be used to offset *unavoidable and material exogenous cost increases* well above the level of the inflation index.

4.   Potential Limitations on Efficiency From Oversight Standards and Monitoring Procedures

The implementation of price level regulation (whether actual or proposed) has thus far been uniformly characterized by a continuing reliance on profit standards as a primary performance measure. What varies among jurisdictions (or proposals), however, is the particular form and likely impact of this oversight standard.

The Vermont legislation[200] provides for a maximum five year contract between the telecommunications firm and the regulatory agency, which may provide for the "elimination or reduction of...rate of return requirements."[201] Nevertheless, during the term of the contract the firm must file monthly rate of return reports. No less than annually the regulatory agency must report to the legislature on the firm's rate of return.

The State reserves the right during the term of the contract to order revisions (should negotiations fail) where certain exogenous changes are found to have created "...either extremely severe economic hardships for the company or a condition that is severly detrimental and contrary to the public good...." Among the specified causative changes that might justify a contract revision are "...unforeseen and significant economic shifts, or changes in technology...." Presumably, these might include major aberrations in the inflation index of the type discussed above.

Of particular interest here is the meaning that might be given to "severely detrimental and contrary to the public good". If the chosen inflation factor should far exceed the cost increases of the firm's actual inputs, both the firm's prices and profits would presumably rise beyond initial contemplation. An "aberrant" price rise clearly unsupported by corresponding cost increases could arguably prove "severely detrimental" to the public good. Would such impact be measured by price alone, or would the presence of abnormal profits add substance to a "detriment" that in itself might only doubtfully justify a contract revision based on price alone? Conversely, what if "changes in technology" (whether generated internally or externally) result in cost reductions well in excess of the productivity deflator? Would the existence of abnormal profits, absent any price increase beyond the reasonable contemplation of the price adjustment formula, be viewed as "severely detrimental" to the public good?

The answer to such questions in Vermont must await the test of experience. In any case, however, the requirement of monthly reports of rate of return will affect the firm in two ways. First, the firm will have a continuing, although perhaps a less intense, incentive to minimize its reported return through manipulation of cost transfers from non-contract to contract markets. Second, the calculation of its return will presumably be subject to the cost allocation methodologies of the regulatory agency.

NTIA's price level proposal included "...a one-time review within three years after the effective date of the initial contract."[202] The intended purpose was to "...ensure that the regulatory contract, as initially developed, has generally worked as planned." As part of the review, the regulated firm would be required to estimate its "...overall return on equity for regulated services, *to the extent possible*...." (Emphasis added.) The return would then be compared "...for example, against the Standard and Poor's index for utilities." This in itself may seem a useful performance measure that doesn't substantially impair the firm's incentives for cost reduction or impose rigid allocation standards. However, the proposal includes the proviso that "If the firm's return is excessive (*e.g.*, more than 2 percent above the benchmark), regulators should require the firm to give up half of those profits through refunds or future service discounts to ratepayers." In addition, where returns are determined to be deficient by the same per cent "...regulators should consider increasing the levels of regulated rates."

In seeking some equitable redistribution of income between the firm and its consumers, NTIA may have ignored the realities involved in the determination of earnings. First, whether to avoid refunds or to obtain future rate increases, the firm's incentives for cost reductions would be blunted in some degree. Moreover, the calculation of earnings for the purpose indicated will inevitably invite controversy as to what degree of exactitude is "possible". The use of FDC methodologies will undoubtedly be urged.

NTIA terms its proposal a "one time review". It may consider such a review to be a practical necessity in smoothing the way to acceptance. NTIA may be unduly optimistic, however, in assuming that a single three year period will permit one-time formulaic adjustments that can operate indefinitely without need of further review. There is no assurance that factors operating in any one period to create unacceptable aberrancies will be substantially the same as those arising in subsequent periods. The form of review NTIA proposes, therefore, may create a precedent harmful to the welfare potential of a price level regime for its duration.

The FCC's tentative oversight proposal also contemplates a three year review that includes the "achieved rate of return".[203] Any resulting adjustments in the price ceilings, however, would be wholly prospective, with no provisions for "amortizing" abnormal or deficient earnings. Future adjustments would primarily reflect achieved productivity rates higher or lower than the formulaic adjustment rate. The FCC appropriately observes, however, that "...the productivity factor should not be changed with every modest change in the rate of return or any other factor...." Where changes are made, the FCC's stated concern is "...that the magnitude of any change not be so great as to recreate the disincentive to further productivity gains, as under rate-of-return regulation."

As compared to NTIA's proposal, the FCC's salutary purpose is to maintain the firm's incentives to efficiency by reducing its risk of losing the resulting benefits. In the matter of intermarket allocative efficiency, however, the FCC's proposal may not offer a significant improvement over traditional profit level regulation. Its AT&T price cap proposal is limited, of course, to that firm's regulated interstate interexchange markets. These must continue to be separated from its similar intrastate markets, many of which are largely deregulated, and from unregulated telecommunications related services. As for local exchange carriers, only interstate carrier "access" services would be under price level regulation, thus requiring separation from all other regulated and unregulated services.

The need to determine an "achieved rate of return" for specific services under price cap regulation will perpetuate the use of current (or similar) methodologies for calculating putative costs in particular markets. The firm's incentives to manipulate cost transfers from unregulated to regulated markets will diminish only slightly, if at all. The FCC's propensity to stymie these efforts through regulatory overkill are likely to persist.

Absent a tradition of rate of return regulation in the United Kingdom, British Telecom is nevertheless subject to an earnings related performance standard monitored by OFTEL. Its Director General is authorized to propose a formula change to the Merger and Monopolies Commission in the event of excessive rates of return. The Director General has stated the following policy for the exercise of this authority:[204]

> ...if it could be demonstrated that, within the constraints offered by the [RPI-3] formula, BT was able to make excessive rates of return for reasons other than exceptional improvements in efficiency, or to support an unreasonable degree of inefficiency, it would be possible to initiate proceedings to secure a review of the formula before 1989.

In his 1985 Annual Report the Director General referred to public complaints about price increases in the past year. Following an *ex parte* investigation of British Telecom's earnings, the Director General found that "...the rate of return on capital employed was probably a little above the minimum acceptable level in competitive capital markets, but it was not so high that I should be justified in interfering less than 18 months after the licence...and about one year after the shares had been sold on that basis."[205]

In the following year the Director General, again in response to complaints, was prompted to review specific earnings for access line services. As reported in the 1986 Annual Report, the preliminary conclusions, based on OFTEL's own investigation (without recourse to public hearings), were that "...BT was not earning excessive profits on these services, that the price increases had been needed to eliminate deficits which had grown up in the past as a result of holding prices below economic levels, but that in the aggregate, prices had now reached their economic level and further large overall increases were not to be expected."[206]

All of the price increases under investigation in these two years were in fact within both the basic RPI-3 formula and British Telecom's "voluntary" RPI+2 limitation on increases for access line rentals. The sole basis for these investigations was in complaints of excessive earnings under the formulas. Given the results of the investigations and the lack of published information regarding the rates of return found by the Director General, it is difficult to evaluate the actual purposes of the exercise. One plausible surmise is that the ongoing review of earnings has a role in the informal negotiations between the firm and its regulator on the annual application of the price adjustment formulas.

This thought finds support in the 1987 year end adjustment period. On that occasion the Director General "... welcomed BT's decision to peg the main charges for controlled services in November 1987 [considering that] the RPI-3 formula would have allowed BT to increase prices of 'basket' services by an average of 1.3 per cent."[207] Although the separate RPI+2 formula would have allowed a further 6.3 per cent increase for the most price inelastic access line charges, no increase was applied. Was the Director General's 1986 statement a declaration of objective financial fact or the product of a prior understanding reached with British Telecom? Or was the price freeze a unilateral political act by the firm out of concern for "excess" earnings in advance of its 1989 license review?

While the freeze applied across all principal markets under price level regulation, one especially noteworthy effect was in the residential access line charge.[208] By this freeze, British Telecom was able to maintain a 20.5% cumulative increase during 1984-87 on the sensitive access line charge, substantially equivalent to the 20.1% cumulative RPI. Whatever its earnings, it could at least point to price increases no greater than the general level of RPI increases.

Concern is reflected in other license requirements for the possible subsidization by British Telecom's regulated sector of its unregulated competitive services (equipment and data enhancement). These requirements include the use of a separate subsidiary for unregulated operations, the maintenance of separate accounts for separate lines of business and the reporting of interbusiness transfer prices and common cost allocations. Other than the use of a separate subsidiary (which does not seem structured to bar the realization of joint and common expense economies), these requirements are largely informational. They do not impose a priori cost allocation formulas.[209]

The past universal use of an earnings test as a performance measure under a price level regime suggests a certain inevitability. Its use can perhaps be justified in the same manner as the productivity deflator of the inflation adjustment: i.e., as the basis for an equitable distribution of benefits from an experimental regulatory regime that imposes certain risks on both firm and consumer. The broader social welfare aim of any such use of earnings as a performance measure, however, must be to effect any appropriate distributions without destroying the source of the surplus that is to be distributed.

5. Problems in Defining the Constitutional Entitlements of Investors and Consumers Under a Price Level Regime

As a departure from traditional cost-based profit level regulation, a price level regime would require the adaptation of established 5th and 14th amendment "confiscation" doctrines to a new setting. A major source of current doctrine is *F.P.C. v. Hope Natural Gas Co.* [210] In *Hope,* the Supreme Court addressed the rights of (i) investors in public utilities subject to government regulation of earnings and restrictions on market abandonment and (ii) consumers made captive for essential services to a governmentally protected monopoly.

Although *Hope* directly involved the "just and reasonable" rate standard of the Natural Gas Act, its rationale has constitutional significance. In positing a basic identity of statutory and constitutional standards, the Court said: "Since there are no constitutional requirements more exacting than the standards of the Act, a rate order which conforms to the latter does not run afoul of the former."[211] The question is whether the essential equivalence between statutory and constitutional standards would remain under a statutory price level regime, or whether earnings related tests would yet be required for constitutional purposes. The issue involves the rights of both the firm (representing its investors) and consumers.

A basic dictum of *Hope* is that "...the fixing of 'just and reasonable' rates, involves a balancing of the investor and consumer interests." The investor's "legitimate concern" is in the "financial integrity" of the firm. As an "end result" of the earnings allowance, this concern requires that "...the return to the equity owner should be commensurate with returns on other industries having corresponding risks [and] sufficient to assure confidence in the financial integrity of the enterprise, so as to maintain its credit and to attract capital."[212]

In protecting the investors of a firm under price level regulation against confiscation, it would seem necessary to retain the essence of

Hope's "end result" doctrine. For a firm subject to constraints on market abandonment, the determination of confiscation requires an assessment of the financial impact of regulation as the initial point of inquiry. Under a price level regime, however, the new balance between the firm's potential risks and gains may prompt some adjustments in the usual decisional standards. In particular, an issue may arise as to whether a firm's new right to generate abnormal profits should be offset by some greater assumption of downside risk. Specifically, in the case of diversified public utilities, courts may become more inclined to require the use of any deeper corporate pockets which may be available to sustain the firm's regulated activities in periods of financial stress.[213] In the case of non-diversified firms serving only in regulated markets, practical financial and economic necessity may create a more immediate need for judicial relief in well founded claims of confiscation. In general, a price level regime should not materially affect a firm's ability to pursue confiscation claims within the broad framework of existing constitutional standards. Of course, to make its case it could be required to satisfy judicially imposed cost determination standards.

Less clear are the constitutional remedies available to consumers under a price level regime. Would "captive" consumers of government protected monopolies enjoy protection against the monopoly's abnormal earnings? What is the nature of the "consumer interest" to be protected under *Hope?*

Following its recital of *Hope's* "just and reasonable" standard "from the company's point of view", one Court of Appeals observed that "From the consumer standpoint no such criteria are available."[214] Subsequent decisions construing the "just and reasonable" standard, however, have provided some gloss. A starting point is this widely cited passage from *Washington Gas Light Co. v. Baker:*[215]

> ...the end of public utility regulation has been recognized to be protection of consumers from exorbitant rates. Thus, there is a zone of reasonableness within which rates may properly fall. It is bounded at one end by the investor interest against confiscation and at the other against exorbitant rates.

Note that protection against exorbitancy is here defined directly in terms of rates paid by consumers rather than returns realized by the firm.[216] In *Permian Basin,*[217] however, the Supreme Court considered whether price differentials under an FPC prescribed two-tier incentive rate plan were consistent with this same "zone of reasonableness" test under the Natural Gas Act. The Court approved the plan with the observation that the "...the two-price rate structure will provide both a useful incentive to exploration and prevent *excessive producer profits.*" (Emphasis added.)

This statement reflects a common practice of defining the consumer entitlement to protection against "exorbitant rates" in terms of the firm's "excessive profits." Nevertheless, the duality of expression poses several questions. First, is the entitlement of consumers under *Hope* measured by the level of rates paid (as compared, perhaps, to some other level of rates); is it measured by the level of the firm's return; or by both? Second, assuming that the standard of "excessive profits" (or returns) provides a major element of consumer protection under current regulation, is such protection uniquely tied to profit level regulation as a matter of logical necessity? Or, like the firm's protection against confiscation, would consumer protection against excessive profits continue even if cost-based regulation were replaced by price level regulation? *In sum, would protection of captive consumers against "excessive profits" remain a necessary constitutional adjunct of price level regulation?*[218]

The answer could lie in a suitable legislative (or administrative) statement of purpose. The problem is to avoid the constitutional impairment of the basic incentive structure of a price level regime from which its principal potential benefits derive. Accordingly, that statement should clearly delineate the anticipated social welfare gains resulting from the unlinking of prices and profits. As noted above, in *Permian Basin* the Supreme Court approved a controversial FPC two-tier price structure intended to provide exploration incentives. In its more general approval of the FPC's entire scheme of area-wide cost determinations and rate prescriptions the Court drew support from the dictum of an earlier landmark decision which had vastly expanded the scope of constitutional price regulation: "Price control is 'unconstitutional...if arbitrary, discriminatory, or demonstrably irrelevant to the policy the legislature is free to adopt....' *Nebbia v. New York*, 291 U.S. 502, 539."[219]

It is possible to conclude that under a properly articulated economic rationale, consumer protection against "excessive profits", as traditionally applied under profit level regulation, could not be invoked to reestablish a necessary link between prices and profits. Nevertheless, as long as regulated firms providing essential services operate as government protected monopolies, with competitive entry barred or severely restricted, it is not likely that consumer protection against confiscation of property through "gross", "egregious" or "unconscionable" prices will be totally abandoned.[220] In effect, therefore, the standard of constitutional protection for consumers under a price level regime would be modified. The focus would shift from protection against "excessive profits" *per se*, as defined under profit level regulation, to protection against prices viewed as "unconscionable" and "demonstrably irrelevant" to the purposes of the price level regime.

Such prices might result from uncorrected price adjustment formulas suffering severe aberrations. These consequences of an errant mechanism should be amenable to judicial review under the statutory process itself. Accordingly, statutory and constitutional standards and processes under a price level regime will likely achieve the same identity as under *Hope*. Both standards will be judicially enforced primarily through the customary review of administrative decisions.

4

Implementing a Price Level Regime for Diversified Public Utilities

A. AS APPLIED TO THE FIRM'S NATURAL MONOPOLY MARKETS

1. Structuring an Efficient Process for Efficacious Decisions

The decisional elements and processes in determining prices under profit and price level regulation differ significantly. Under profit level regulation the (indirect) price decision is largely a product of regulatory discretion in reducing a welter of competing variables and interests into a politically acceptable decision that projects a sufficient aura of rationality. To these ends the opportunities for obscured tradeoffs are legion. If the desired result requires a rate of return that seems too high or too low, then the same result can be reached by use of a different rate of return with compensating adjustments in operating costs or the rate base. If the rate base is the sensitive issue, then a more satisfying or less vulnerable result can be achieved through adjustments in the rate of return. Similarly, the impact of economically improvident decisions on the allowance or disallowance of controversial operating costs can be eased through adjustments in the rate base or rate of return. Where the result proves unpalatable the parties can return to the regulatory drawing board.

In contrast to the broad discretion available to justify a given decision under profit level regulation, the direct price decision under price level regulation is largely automatic—a product of predetermined formulas. It is this comparative absence of regulatory discretion (whether employed for better or worse) that increases the need to infuse the best possible economic content into the selection and administration of the price formula.[221] The need is for the highest possible quality of decisions on issues of critical importance to the efficacious operation of a price level regime. "Satisficing" rather than "optimizing" though such decisions must be, they should reflect the greatest degree of economic objectivity consistent with political acceptability.[222] To that end the most critical decisions under a price level regime should be divorced as much as possible from economically irrational influences, including the usual tradeoffs of the regulatory process. What can not be eliminated, however, are the needs for basic due process and political oversight.

One model for determining the various elements of a price level regime is found in the development of British Telecom's license. British Telecom has described the process as follows:

> The BT Licence was granted on 22 June 1984 for a period of at least twenty five years. The text was drafted by the Government (Dept. of Trade and Industry) before Oftel was formally created, in negotiation with BT and was designed to balance the needs of competitors, customers and the public against the need of the potential shareholders who would soon be asked to buy shares in the new company.[223]

This model of direct private negotiations between firm and government is hardly a candidate for adoption in the United States. While it meets the tests of efficiency and direct political oversight, it fails the test of due process. The task then is to identify a process congenial to legal standards and expectations in the United States that might best be used to determine the elements of a price level scheme for any given firm, or for an industry sector within a given jurisdiction. One possibility for merging greater economic objectivity with due process and political responsibility would be in a combination of interest arbitration and regulatory oversight for at least some "introductory" period.[224]

Under such an arrangement the fact finding function and the presumptively final determination of the substantive provisions of a particular price level regime (or contract) would be committed to a panel of independent economic experts. The basic decisional guidelines would derive from the economic goals of the governing statute, perhaps as further articulated by the regulatory agency following an expedited presentation of views by interested parties. These guidelines should be sufficiently specific to provide some identifiable constraint on the panel's discretion. Equally important, the guidelines must be broad enough to permit rational choices among economic alternatives.

The panel's principal responsibility would be to prescribe the basic elements of the price adjustment formula. These include: the inflation factor; the productivity deflator; the inclusion (or exclusion) in the price adjustment formula of demand related variables, and the character of any to be included; the price structure, including "baskets", weighting factors and any special constraints on the range of particular price movements; and standards for determining non-programmed price adjustments attributable to unforeseen exogenous cost or demand changes.

As in the case of interest arbitration awards (as well as interpretive awards), panel decisions filling in these critical components of a price level scheme would in essence be final. Political oversight would be retained through authority of the regulatory agency to set aside and remand (or modify) the "award", in whole or in part, for evident failure to comply with the guidelines or for any material attributes that might be fairly viewed as "arbitrary or capricious." What the regulatory agency would lack is authority to set aside or modify the award because of disagreement with arbitral judgments. In effect, the basic legislative delegation of decisional authority would be to the arbitral panel, subject to this reserve authority of the regulatory agency.[225]

There is little reason to assume that the work products of informed experts will perform flawlessly.[226] Nevertheless, in initiating an era (or an experimental period) of price level regulation, a realistic effort to reduce the risks of failure seems justified. The proposal is not a sharp departure from the model of an administrative law judge as fact finder and author of an initial recommendation. The difference lies mainly in the degree of finality of the initial proposal. That difference is justified by the added expertise of the panel and perhaps by its greater sensitivity to the opinions of its professional peers. Perpetuation of this special, and perhaps more costly, decisional process should be less necessary following the establishment of an initial pattern of decisions. That pattern could provide useful guidance for the future application of economic doctrine by regulators to the initiation of additional price level schemes.

2. Maintaining Efficiency Incentives Through Minimal Recourse to Profit Level Standards

The point has been made and repeated that the potential contributions of price level regulation to productive and allocative efficiency could be severely eroded by failure to achieve an effective unlinking of the firm's revenues and profits from its internal costs. Necessary support for such unlinking, however, may be difficult to achieve. The pervasive public association of consumer welfare with the prevention of abnormal profits in regulated markets militates toward retention of profit level standards as a primary measure of performance.

One important question in structuring an efficacious price level scheme is whether an acceptable surrogate for profit levels in the regulated sector can be devised as a measure of consumer welfare. The need is for a measure that can (i) command credibility; (ii) preserve incentives to productive efficiency and (iii) free the firm and its prices from the economically irrelevant rigidities of "fully distributed" cost allocations.

The ultimate credible and acceptable measure of consumer equity should theoretically be found in comparisons of prices generated under price level regulation with those which would have obtained under continuing profit level regulation. The proposed use of CPI as an easily grasped cost inflation index offers the special appeal of immediate comparisons between changes in regulated prices and general price levels. Even if such comparisons were favorable, their acceptance as a measure of consumer welfare could quickly evaporate if further data also established that historical relationships in changes between profit level prices and the CPI were even more favorable to consumers.

If (for the moment) comparable service quality is assumed, the real measure of consumer welfare is not found in comparisons of current price/CPI changes, but in whether prices are lower than they would otherwise have been. Can a system be devised for producing reliable and credible price predictions? The undertaking is far from simple, but its ingredients should be considered for further study.

The analysis is necessarily counterfactual—that is, a consideration of what would have been. As suggested above, it involves the comparison of an observed price path over a period of time under price level regulation with a projected price path under the former regime over the same period. If "observed" prices were below "projected" prices, the argument could be made that consumers were indeed better off under the new regime.

This determination, if it is feasible at all, requires a model that relates the price observed under the old regime to an index of economic variables regularly confronted by the firm and the regulator (of which the CPI may be only one). This model would then serve as the theoretical basis for a statistical study of the relationships among these variables.

For purpose of discussion consider again the single product firm. Assume that under the former regime the firm attempts to maximize its profits to whatever degree possible under the profit level constraint. Among the available means may be the price of its output, subject to any regulatory constraint. To the extent that the firm can choose a price, that price is "endogenous" to it.

The exact choice of the output price will depend on factors other than the regulatory constraint. For example, factors affecting demand will affect the price the firm will set for its product. Such demand factors would include general price and income levels in the firm's service area and of prices for other particular goods and services. These factors are all outside the control of the regulated firm, or "exogenous" to it. The important point is that within regulatory constraints the level of the endogenous variable (i.e., price) will be adapted to the level(s) of the exogenous variables affecting demand.

In addition, the choice of price will depend on variables affecting the firm's costs of providing service. These would include wage rates, the cost of capital (e.g., the interest rate at which the firm can borrow money) and fuel and raw material prices. These factor price variables are largely outside the control of the regulated firm, and to that extent are also "exogenous" to it.

Technological factors beyond the firm's control, such as exogenous increases in productivity, can also affect the firm's costs. Thus, a new technological innovation, such as fiber optics or superconductive networks, may lower the firm's costs and affect its choice of output price. In sum, the level of an endogenous variable such as price will be influenced by the levels of the exogenous variables affecting demand and cost (including exogenous productivity increases).

Having identified the exogenous variables affecting price, the analyst could proceed to the second step—the use of a regression analysis to study the statistical relationship between price and the exogenous variables. In other words using data from the "old" regulatory regime, the analysis would show how output prices were related to the exogenous variables in the economic system before the transition to price level regulation.

Operationally this might entail a regression of output price on variables such as factor prices (or a proxy such as PPI); the rate of exogenous technical change in this industry; a measure of income in the relevant market (deflated by a measure of the general price level such as the CPI or the GNP deflator); and the prices of substitute or complementary goods and services. The regression would utilize data drawn from a suitable period before the transition to price level regulation.

The third step would be to use the quantitative relationship derived in the second step to project the post-transition prices that might have been observed had the old regime continued. The analyst would use data on the exogenous variables from the post-transition period in the same statistical relationship estimated for the pre-transition period.

Finally, the analyst would compare the projected price with the observed price under price level regulation. As with all statistical studies, the projected price will not be predicted with certainty. The prediction will therefore include both a price estimate and the degree of uncertainty associated with it. Through use of observations on the exogenous variables in the post-transition period, the analyst would be able to construct a range of prices falling within a specified confidence interval (e.g., the 95% confidence interval). The smaller the confidence interval, the more certain the measure of the projected price level. The analyst would then be able to conclude whether the observed price (under price level regulation) falls within, above or below the confidence interval associated with the projected price.

The discussion suggests the importance of using all relevant exogenous variables. Any omitted variable may contain information that is important for predictive purposes, especially if that variable is not highly correlated with variables that are included in the prediction process. The failure to consider carefully for inclusion in the index any exogenous variable that theory suggests may be important would create a pitfall.

This discussion dealing with a single product firm is deliberately simplified. Extensions of the same basic methodology to more complicated regulatory environments are also possible. If the firm produces two or more products, each endogenously determined price would be a function of its own exogenous parameters. A set of output prices covering the relationship between price and the exogenous variables for each service could be estimated simultaneously. The same methodology could also be extended to multi-part tariffs. Consider the case of a single product with a previously described two-part tariff. As was noted, the access charge can be viewed as the price for one service and the message unit rate as the price for another. These separate prices could also be estimated simultaneously.

Such comparisons of observed and projected prices for multiple services or multi-part tariffs could prove especially complicated. For example, suppose the observed price for the monthly access charge is higher than the projected price, but the message unit charge is lower. Are consumers better off under the new price level regime? The answer is not immediately obvious. Some may be; others may not. Further resort to some index of weighted prices may assist in the comparison; but for scientific validation, its particular construction would require some theoretical justification.

Nor, in the end, can the quality of service under price level regulation be ignored in comparing observed and projected prices. Consumer welfare under the two regulatory regimes must in theory encompass service quality as well as price. If quality were chosen by the firm endogenously under the old regime, and a measure (or an index) of service quality exists, a regression of service quality could be performed on the same exogenous variables identified in the price projection study. A "projected service quality" could then be predicted for the post-transition period. This projection could then be compared with the observed quality of service under price level regulation.[227]

In some cases such joint comparisons may lead to fairly clear conclusions. If, for example, observed price is lower than projected price and observed quality is at least as high as projected quality, then consumer welfare has increased under the price level regime. However, the results will not always be so clear. If, for example, the observed price and service quality were both lower than the projections, the result would be ambiguous without further knowledge about consumer preferences regarding price and quality in the relevant range.

The theoretical appeal of measuring consumer welfare through comparing observed and projected prices and service quality may ultimately give way to practical impediments. But the potential benefits to be realized from price performance standards not linked to the firm's costs and profits are substantial. Their possible realization warrants continuing consideration.

Where political considerations do require a profit based measure of price performance, the measure should be so structured as to minimize resulting inefficiencies. One important element of such a structure would be the limitation of the profit standard to the firm's overall earnings in the regulated sector. Determining profits for each of the various services rendered through shared facilities and common costs would require the same arbitrary cost allocation procedures that have deterred demand oriented pricing under profit level regulation.

In theory, the separation of costs between the regulated and unregulated markets of diversified firms would also seem to require these same allocation mechanisms. The purpose of determining profit levels in regulated markets under price level regulation, however, differs significantly from the purpose under profit level regulation. The purpose under the latter is to determine costs as the necessary basis for a revenue allowance. An appearance of precision in cost determination is required, however illusory in fact. Under price level regulation the principal regulatory purpose in determining overall earnings in the firm's regulated sector is for general comparison. Rather than separating costs in regulated and unregulated markets by prescribed allocations intended to control costs and prices in the regulated markets, such separations should be effected through methods consistent with generally accepted accounting principles (GAAP).

The maintenance of accounts on a consistent basis under GAAP should indicate the amount and trend of the firm's overall regulated earnings and return on equity.[228] The presence of grossly abnormal or seriously deficient earnings sufficient to warrant a review of existing price levels would be revealed. What might be still avoided, or minimized, is a direct link between the firm's revenues and costs.[229] Such an arrangement may not sever the link permanently; but it may extend a period of "regulatory lag" long enough to maintain productive efficiency as a central goal in the firm's ongoing incentive structure. That is to say, the firm's risk of losing the benefits of internal cost reduction may become sufficiently remote to justify the continuing effort.

B. AS APPLIED TO RELATIONSHIPS BETWEEN THE DIVERSIFIED FIRM'S REGULATED AND UNREGULATED MARKETS

1. Responsibilities of the Diversified Firm for the Provision of Natural Monopoly Services

The usual incentive for a firm to diversify is the expectation of financial gain. Where the expectation is realized (and all else being equal), the natural monopoly markets of a diversified public utility will benefit from improvements in the firm's financial condition. Under price level regulation any resulting reduction in capital costs or improvements in the terms and conditions of acquiring supplies will not operate to lower rates in the natural monopoly markets. But the firm's added financial strength can be utilized to support its service commitments in these markets.

Concern for the financial integrity of regulated services requires that relations between the firm's regulated and unregulated markets be premised on the reality that diversification can weaken as well as strengthen its financial condition. Where the incentive to diversify is revenue or asset maximization rather than profit maximization, there may be no expectations of financial gain to be realized. Where profits provide the spur, expectations may prove illusory. Where gains are in fact realized, it may be at the cost of improvident asset withdrawals from regulated markets. In short, whatever the potential gains from diversification for the firm and its regulated markets, they are accompanied by corresponding risk.

In structuring relations between the diversified firm's regulated and unregulated markets under price level regulation it is essential to distinguish between (i) separating the costs of regulated and unregulated services for rate making and (ii) maintaining the firm's financial ability to meet its service obligations. The proper guideline is that the diversified firm should be as free as any other firm operating in unregulated markets to pursue its lawful entrepreneurial goals, subject only to its ultimate responsibility for the continuing quality and service coverage of the regulated services.

An approach to (although not a model for) such a arrangement is suggested by "The Capital Adequacy Guidelines for Bank Holding Companies and State Member Banks" established by the Federal Reserve Board under the Bank Holding Company Act.[230] Under the Act bank holding companies are allowed limited diversification into nonbanking, but bank related, activities.[231] The FRB's "Guidelines" impose minimum "total" and "primary" capital to total asset ratios on bank holding companies as well as banks. In effect, the holding companies, including their nonbanking activities on a consolidated basis, must maintain a sufficient capital base in the interest of the enterprise and its bank operations.

The Guidelines provide, however, that "...the degree of leverage common in banking should not automatically extend to nonbanking activities." Instead, "...nonbank subsidiaries of a banking organization should maintain levels of capital consistent with the levels that have been established by industry norm or standards, by Federal or State regulatory agencies for similar firms...or that may be established by the Board after taking into account risk factors of a particular industry." Overall, "...an institution's consolidated capital position should at least equal the sum of the capital requirements of the organization's bank and nonbank subsidiaries as well as those of the parent company."

The point to be made is not that a capital asset ratio is the best, or should be the principal, measure of the financial capability of a diversified public utility. The relevance of the FRB requirements lies in two principles: (i) the diversified firm has ultimate responsibility for the obligation of service in the regulated markets and (ii) protective financial standards should be shaped to relate to, but not exceed, the degree of risk imposed. The following proposals draw on these principles and certain of British Telecom's license conditions.[232]

(i) The diversified firm will operate in accordance with GAAP and may be required by the regulatory agency to meet reasonable balance sheet and liquidity standards intended to assure its ability to fulfil its service obligations in regulated markets. These standards will relate to an objective assessment of the risk associated with the firm's market structure and operations. To implement this obligation, the firm will be required to file periodic reports on its overall financial condition. As reasonably required by the financial condition of the affiliate(s) providing regulated services, the diversified firm may be required to transfer or pledge assets to the affiliate(s).

(ii) A Uniform System of Accounts may be required for the regulated services. The allocation of joint and common expenses between regulated and unregulated markets and among specific regulated services shall be made on a reasonable basis. The firm may be required to file its allocation methods with the regulatory agency to permit the monitoring of changes and consistency with GAAP.

Separate balance sheets, profit and loss statements and related financial data will be maintained for the regulated services of the firm. These will be determined in accordance with applicable FASB standards.[233]

(iii) Material asset transfers (including dividend distributions in cash or property) from regulated to unregulated affiliates will not require prior approval, but will be subject to prior notice requirements and the investigative authority of the regulatory agency. As to any such transaction, the public utility and the diversified firm may be required to show that its effect will not be to impair the ability of the public utility to meet its service obligations. Any assets transferred, following the receipt within a reasonable period of a notice of investigation from the regulatory agency, will be held by the transferee, subject to a determination that the transfer was appropriate or should be rescinded.

The intent of these relationships is to impose responsibility on the diversified firm commensurate with any reasonably perceived added risk to the financial integrity and operating capability of the regulated services. These responsibilities may well introduce a further element of caution into diversification planning, but should not deter the implementation of well considered plans. The proposed relationships would not impose constraints on efficient pricing policies, nor would they require the arbitrary diseconomies of "tributes" from unregulated markets as a condition for diversification.[234]

2. The Regulator's Antitrust Role in the Diversified Firm's Unregulated Markets

It is not the purpose here to evaluate the efficacy of the roles currently assigned to public utility regulators and antitrust agencies in the enforcement of antitrust laws (either in regulated markets or unregulated competitive markets). The sole purpose is to consider how the role of the public utility regulator in unregulated markets should be adapted to a price level regime.

What are the particular antitrust concerns arising from the diversified firm's operations in both market sectors? These are illustrated in the sales by an electric or gas utility of connecting appliances such as stoves or refrigerators.

1. *The utility might use its monopoly power to bar system connections for all appliances not bought from it.* While this tie-in requirement clearly transgresses antitrust standards, it is fully and appropriately amenable to regulatory control as an aspect of the utility's obligation to serve. The change from profit to price level regulation would not affect the issue.

2. *The utility might promote appliance sales through price discounts on utility services to buyers of its appliances.* This too could be reached through antitrust restraints on tie-ins and discrimination, but again would be properly and effectively dealt with through customary regulatory prohibitions on unreasonable price discrimination. The change in regulatory regimes would not affect the issue.[235]

3. *The utility might market, install and service its appliances through personnel and facilities used in common with its provision of utility services. The utility might then be able to support or subsidize its competitive appliance operations through disproportionate assignments of joint and common costs to its regulated markets.* Under profit level regulation this possibility engenders vigorous regulatory efforts to control intermarket cost transfers. This primary regulatory concern

for excessive cost attribution to the regulated sector intersects with an antitrust concern for resulting predation in the unregulated appliance market. Because the regulator's direct concern with intermarket cost transfers is entwined with antitrust concerns, the primary regulatory concern may extend to ancillary antitrust considerations.

Under price level regulation any legitimate regulatory concern for higher rates resulting from excessive cost transfers to the regulated market would disappear. With it should be eliminated any antitrust enforcement role for the regulator in the competitive appliance market. If issues of predatory pricing arise, they should be resolved through marginal cost based standards and applicable antitrust doctrines. The regulator's traditional recourse to fully distributed cost methodologies should have no role under price level regulation. Nor do regulators have any particular expertise in determining the marginal costs of unregulated activities. There is no reason in this respect to commit antitrust enforcement in unregulated competitive markets to the regulatory process where the firm engaged in the unregulated activity is subject to price level regulation in its natural monopoly markets.

4. *Absent joint and common costs, the regulated firm may use financial resources acquired through regulated activities in support of its unregulated activities to a degree that results in predation.* In theory, this concern could be exacerbated under price level regulation because of the absence of profit constraints.

Profit level regulation seeks to limit internally generated funds after operating expenses, taxes and interest to amounts necessary for dividend payouts and reinvestment for utility purposes. To the extent that funds are inappropriately reinvested in unregulated rather regulated activities, the regulator may intervene in support of utility operations. This regulatory concern for the utility's financial ability to meet service obligations will be the same under either form of regulation.[236] This is a regulatory rather than an antitrust concern. In itself it provides no better rationale for regulatory intervention in behalf of antitrust enforcement in unregulated markets than do the concerns for predation in Item 3, above.

In sum, the four categories discussed above fall into two broad groupings—issues of (i) non-discriminatory access to and pricing of the regulated services and (ii) the potential subsidization of anticompetitive conduct in unregulated markets through preferential transfer transactions from, or the absorption of costs by, the regulated markets.

In the case of category (i) issues, the presence of antitrust concerns can not foreclose regulatory conduct in support of a primary interest to remove the discrimination (and, in consequence, the restraints on competition as well). In the case of category (ii) issues, the role of the regulator should be limited to what is reasonably required to protect the financial integrity of the regulated markets.

Under profit level regulation the regulator may feel compelled to allocate costs in an effort to lower the revenue allowance in direct defense of consumer prices. In so doing, the regulator may appear to assume a legitimate secondary antitrust function. Under price level regulation any need for that function in support of regulated prices is essentially eliminated. What remains is a more general concern for financial integrity. This continuing role in behalf of the regulated sector can be discharged without the assumption of any antitrust enforcement role in competitive markets.[237] That role is better left to the more consistent cost standards of a single regulatory regime.

Conclusion

The initiation of price level regulation for the natural monopoly markets of diversified public utilities would have three main aims. Each could prove attainable under a properly structured regime that effectively unlinks the firm's internal costs from its revenue allowance.

The first is to assure cost efficient public utility services of suitable quality, with the benefits of greater productive efficiency ultimately shared by the utility and its consumers. The second is to promote allocative efficiency through pricing that better reflects both marginal costs and elasticities of demand. The third is to permit, at less cost and subject to antitrust constraints, a freer development of diversified public utility enterprises better able to realize any available benefits of scope economies, risk diversification and market synergies.

The foregoing discussion of this proposal as applied to the natural monopoly markets of electric, natural gas, telephone, water and common carrier pipeline firms is necessarily general in nature. A price level regime must be structured in relation to the cost characteristics, demand conditions and established service categories of each particular industry. What can not be ignored in any industry sector, however, are the substantial problems, which have been noted, in implementing a suitable scheme for realizing the potential benefits of price level regulation. Perhaps the greatest single barrier to such realization would lie in continuing public insistence on measuring consumer welfare by profits rather than comparative prices.

In this crucial respect, the recently negotiated change in British Telecom's initial "RPI-3" formula to "RPI-4 1/2" is of particular interest.[238] The change, which becomes effective in July, 1989 on expiration of the current formula, was agreed to by OFTEL and British Telecom following the originally contemplated review in late 1988 of the firm's operating and financial experience.

As of this writing a formal rationale for the change has not been announced. Informally, however, British Telecom describes the formula revision as a specific reflection of *projected* productivity gains resulting from current and continuing modernization programs rather than as a general limitation on earnings.[239]

If such is the case, then OFTEL is to be commended, especially for not converting the productivity factor into a mechanism for expropriating a larger share of the firm's efficiency gains from prior periods. If such restraint has in fact been exercised, there remains the question of whether it would be replicated under the political environment for public utility pricing in the United States. The ultimate ability of price level regulation to generate its potential benefits would depend importantly on the refusal of regulators to judge its success or failure primarily by comparative profit levels rather than comparative price levels. Absent such resolve, these benefits could be lost. In natural monopoly markets the efficiency incentives of a price level regime would be dampened. In the case of diversified public utilities, fully distributed costing would continue to distort prices and management decisions both in regulated and unregulated markets.

End Notes

1. A flavor of public utility diversification developments and re-
sulting regulatory issues is found in numerous Public Utilities
Fortnightly articles, of which a few are: Smartt, "Why Regulators
Take a Hard Look at Utility Diversification Plans" 108 PUF No. 6, 6
(1981); Ferrar, "Business Diversification: An Option Worth
Considering", 110 PUF No.1, 13 (1982); Lewis and Ross, "A Road
Map for Utility Diversification", 110 PUF No.13, 17 (1982); Burkhard
and Skrainka, "CP National Corporation - A Case Study In
Diversification", 117 PUF No.7, 39 (1986); Murray and Closterman,
"How Utilities Are Becoming New Con-glomerates", 118 PUF No.3, 11
(1986); Malko and Edgar, "Energy Utility Diversification: Its Status
In Wisconsin", 118 PUF No.3, 20 (1986); Klausing, "Diversification In
the Gas Industry: A Two-Edged Sword", 119 PUF No.13, 27 (1987).
    A broad review of the issues from the perspective of regulators is
found in the "Report of the Ad Hoc Committee on Utility Diversification", Proceedings of the 94th National Association of Regulatory
Utility Commissioners Annual Convention 863-996 (1982) From the
same proceedings, see also the panel discussion "Utility Diversi-fica-
tion: Management Desires Versus Regulatory Concerns", Concurrent
Business Session A 41, Nov. 11, 1982. An equivalent review from an
industry perspective appears in "Diversification in the Utility
Industry", Cabot Consulting Group, Final Report (Mar., 1982). A focal
point for diversification developments and issues within the telecom-
munications industry is provided by the Modified Final Judgment in
the AT&T divestiture proceedings (*infra*, nn. 33 and 35) and in FCC
Computer II and III proceedings. *Infra*, n. 39 and related text. In
general see: DIVERSIFICATION, DEREGULATION, AND
INCREASED UNCERTAINTY IN THE PUBLIC UTILITY
INDUSTRIES, ed. Trebing, H., Michigan State University Public
Utilities Papers, 1983.
    2. National Telecommunications Information Administration,
NTIA Report (July, 1987) ("NTIA Report"). The proceeding was initi-

ated by a "Notice and Request for Comments", Docket No. 61091-6191, 51 Fed. Reg. 36837 (1986).

3.   "In the Matter of Policy and Rules Concerning Rates for Dominant Carriers", FCC, *Notice of Proposed Rule Making*, Adopted: Aug. 4, 1987; Released: Aug. 21, 1987, CC Docket No. 87-313, FCC Docket No. 87-263, 2 FCC Rcd 5208. Fed. Reg. publication, without notes, 52 FR 33962 (1987) ("Initial Notice").

4.   In characterizing cost allocation rules as "at best imperfect" in preventing cross subsidies, the FCC suggests that rate of return regulation may actually legitimize the firm's overrecovery in regulated markets. Price level regulation, however, "...would substantially decrease incentives to shift costs from more to less competitive service offerings." Initial Notice, *supra*, n. 3, 2 FCC Rcd. 5211, 5213.

"The approach, in short, tends to reduce many of the cross-subsidization problems some perceive when regulated firms operate in both competitive and noncompetitive markets, even if they do not always eliminate those concerns altogether." NTIA Report, *supra*, n. 2, 38.

5.   *Further Notice of Proposed Rulemaking*, CC Docket No. 87-313, FCC Docket No. 88-172, May 23, 1988 ("Further Notice").

6.   Title 30, Vermont Stats. Ann., §§ 226a and 227a. The 1987 proposal by the Oregon Public Utility Commissioner is set out in Appendices "A" and "B" , Oregon P.U.C. Order No. 87-014 (Jan. 7, 1987).

7.   Telecommunications Act 1984.

8.   The definitive rules governing British Telecom's operations are in its license. "Licence granted by The Secretary of State for Trade and Industry to British Telecommunication under Section 7 of the Telecommunications Act 1984, as amended to July 31, 1987 (London, H.M.S.O. 1987) (License). For further discussion of the British Telecom model See: *British Telecom Comments to FCC Notices of Inquiry and of Proposed Rulemaking*, 2 FCC Rcd. 1022, CC Dkt. No. 86-494 (1987) and in the Initial Notice, *supra*, n. 3. See also: *Comments of the Office of Telecommunications* ("OFTEL") (British) in NTIA's "Notice; Request for Comments", *Comprehensive Review of Rate of Return Regulation of the U.S. Telecommunications Industry*, 51 Fed. Reg. 36837, Docket No. 61091-6191 (Oct. 16, 1986). (This notice initiated the proceeding resulting in the NTIA Report, *supra*, n. 2.)

The origins of the British Telecom arrangement and a useful description and appraisal are found in Bhattacharyya and Laughhunn, "Price Cap Regulation: Can We Learn From the British Experience?", 120 PUF No. 8, 11 (1987). (cited as Bhattacharyya.)

9. In addressing the *economic* rationale for regulation, this section does not deal with the *politics* of regulation.

10. F.M. Scherer, INDUSTRIAL MARKET STRUCTURE AND ECONOMIC PERFORMANCE 482 (1980). For another description of the view prevailing before widespread regulatory reform, see A.Kahn, THE ECONOMICS OF REGULATION: PRINCIPLES, Vol. 1 (1970).

11. As a technical point, it is the concept of subadditivity of costs rather than economies of scale that determines whether an industry is a natural monopoly. A cost structure is said to be subadditive for a given level of output if it is less costly for a single firm, as opposed to any group of two or more firms, to produce the output. Economies of scale are neither necessary nor sufficient for a natural monopoly. For more on the concepts of economies of scale and subadditivity, see W.J. Baumol, J.C. Panzer, and R.D. Willig, CONTESTABLE MARKETS AND THE THEORY OF INDUSTRY STRUCTURE (Rev. Ed. 1988).

12. A possible fourth model is outright deregulation. A case for this model (combined with the taxation of excess profits) is presented in Posner, "Natural Monopoly and Its Regulation", 21 Stan. L. Rev. 548 (1969), and critiqued in "Comments" and "Reply", 2 Stan L. Rev. 510-546 (1970).

13. See Demsetz, "Why Regulate Utilities?" 11 J. of Law and Econ. 55-65 (1968). In order for auction competition to allocate resources efficiently, two conditions mst be satisfied. First, inputs must be available to all bidders in open markets at competitively determined prices. Second, the cost of collusion among bidding rivals must be prohibitively high, so that competitive bidding is in fact the outcome of the bidding process.

14. See, for example, Goldberg. "Regulation and Administered Contracts," 7 Bell J. of Econ. 426-448 (1976) and Williamson, "Franchise Bidding for Natural Monopolies—In General and with Respect to CATV," 7 Bell J. of Econ. 73-104 (1976).

15. The theory of contestability is developed in Baumol, Panzar and Willig, *supra*, n. 11.

16. A Full and formal discussion of sunk costs is beyond the scope of this paper. For more on this topic see Baumol, Panzar and Willig, *Id.* at 280-281, and Braeutigam, "Optimal Policies for Natural Monopolies", in Richard Schmalensee and Robert D. Willig, ed., forthcoming HANDBOOK OF INDUSTRIAL ORGANIZATION, North Holland: Amsterdam, The Netherlands.

17. For more on monopolistic competition, see, for example, E. Chamberlin, THE THEORY OF MONOPOLISTIC COMPETITION (8th Ed., 1962).

18. To understand why regulation might be warranted in these circumstances consider the single product firm earning a normal profit under competition for the market. If the firm is charging the same price to all users, then the price charged by the firm will equal average cost. In economic parlance, such a price is considered to be "second best". An even more efficient "first best" price would equal marginal (rather than average) cost. The implementation of a first best pricing scheme, however, may require subsidies to the firm or some form of price discrimination. These more complicated pricing schemes may prove too complex for implementation under competition for the market. If the efficiency gains of first best relative to second best are large enough, then regulation may be implemented as a means of inducing the industry to perform more efficiently. For a discussion of the possibility of more efficient pricing schemes under regulation see Braeutigam (forthcoming), *supra,* n. 16, and S.J. Brown, and D.S. Sibley, THE THEORY OF PUBLIC UTILITY PRICING (1986).

19. For more on the measure of consumer and producer surplus, see Willig, "Consumer's Surplus Without Apology", 66 Amer. Econ. Rev. 589-97 (1976).

20. Several of these properties are demonstrated in R.R. Braeutigam *"Diversification of Natural Monopolies into Competitive Markets"* (April, 1988) (unpublished manuscript). That analysis considers the case in which the firm diversifies into a competitive market, i.e., a market in which the regulated firm cannot affect the market price by its actions. (It would be possible, of course, to construct models in which the firm *can* affect the market price in the competitive market.)

21. One might normally believe that even with diversification the firm would fail to break even with marginal cost pricing in all markets, including both monopoly and competitive markets. In that case one might wish to find the output levels that maximize net economic benefit subject to a breakeven constraint. The firm would then produce output so that the marginal cost in the competitive market equals the competitive market price. See Braeutigam (unpublished manuscript), *supra,* n. 20.

22. See E.E. Zajac, FAIRNESS OR EFFICIENCY: AN INTRODUCTION TO PUBLIC UTILITY PRICING (1978) and Faulhaber, "Cross-Subsidization: Pricing in Public Enterprises", 65 Amer. Econ. Rev. 966 (1975).

23. Averch and Johnson, "Behavior of the Firm under Regulatory Constraint", 52 Amer. Econ. Rev. 1053 (1962). For more on the Averch

NOTES TO CHAPTER 1   PAGES 9-12

and Johnson analysis see Kahn, *supra*, n. 10. See also, E.E. Bailey, ECONOMIC THEORY OF REGULATORY CONSTRAINT (1973).

24. When the allowed rate of return equals the cost of capital in the Averch and Johnson formulation, the firm attempts to maximize profit subject to the constraint that profit is less than or equal to zero. In that case the firm will be indifferent to any point of operation at which it can earn zero profit.

25. An inelastic region of demand is any portion of the demand schedule along which a reduction in price leads to a reduction in total revenue because of the failure of demand to increase by as large a percentage as the price reduction.

26. See, for example, Joskow and Noll, "Regulation in Theory and Practice: An Overview," in STUDIES IN PUBLIC REGULATION, 1-65 (G. Fromm ed. 1981).

27. Skepticism is expressed for a model that is critically dependent in logical development on an assumed difference between the allowed return and cost of capital. See Joskow "Inflation and Environmental Concern: Structural Change in the Process of Public Utility Regulation," 2 J. Law & Econ. 291 (1974).

28. Such a model is considered in Braeutigam, R.R. and Panzar, J.C., "Diversification Incentives Under 'Price-Based' and 'Cost Based' Regulation", 1988, manuscript. As a matter of termininology, the distinction between "core" and "noncore" markets will also be used more broadly to distinguish between the regulated and unregulated markets of a diversified firm.

29. The following examples are among the possible principles by which a regulator might require the common costs of core and noncore services to be allocated: (i) for a telephone firm, in proportion to the number of message-minute-miles of each service; (ii) for a railroad, in proportion to the ton-miles or car-miles of each service or (iii) in any industry, in proportion to the attributable costs of each service.

30. As an added note, the firm in these circumstances may have an incentive to choose an inefficient technology. Thus, it may opt for a technology with larger portion of costs attributable to a core service than would be cost minimizing. The incentive for such a choice would be to relieve pressure from the revenue requirement constraint in the core market. This suggests that input inefficiencies may still exist, even though the allowed rate of return equals the actual cost of capital. This would be inconsistent with goal (1).

31. There may also be an incentive to reduce cost in a core market because of "regulatory lag", i.e., the delay between the time at which

the firm succeeds in lowering cost and the time at which enforcement of the regulatory constraint leads to a price reduction. See, *infra*, n. 119 and related text.

32. For a formal treatment of these points see Braeutigam and Panzar, *supra*, n. 28.

33. *U.S. v. Western Electric Co.*, 592 F. Supp. 846, 862 (1984). Similar concerns of state regulators are voiced in the proceedings of the 94th Annual Convention of the National Association of Regulatory Utility Commissioners, 1982. See, Report of the Ad Hoc Committee on Utility Diversification, *supra*, n. 1.

No attempt is made here to assess the social and economic consequences of public utility diversification, whether under profit or price level regulation. In the case of firms operating as regulated natural monopolies, the premise is that freedom to enter into advantageous market combinations offering beneficial cost reductions, risk diversification and marketing synergies should be limited only by (i) constraints which are realistically founded on the firm's undertaking in its regulated monopoly operations to provide reliable service of appropriate quality at reasonable prices and (ii) adherence to antitrust standards.

34. 592 F. Supp. 853. This passage involves the core of the proceeding as the modification of an antitrust decree relating to AT&T's operations in competitive telecomunications markets. However substantial were Judge Greene's concerns for minimizing the role of the decree itself in raising rates for basic telephone services, his most direct responsibility was for the protection of competition in unregulated markets. But, cf., *infra*, nn. 77-79 and related text.

35. *U.S. v. AT&T*, 552 F. Supp. 131, 194 (1982).

36. *U.S. v. Western Electric*, 592 F. Supp. 846 (1984).

37. *Re Mountain States Telephone and Telegraph Co.*, 86 PUR 4th 586 (1987). Others of the numerous state regulatory decisions to the same effect include *Re Mountain States Telephone and Telegraph Co.*, 69 PUR 4th 683 (1985) (Colorado) and 71 PUR 4th 598 (1985) (Utah); *North Carolina v. Southern Bell T.& T.*, 299 S.E.2d 763 (1983). This type of proceeding often involves the procedural issue of whether the telephone company is authorized to transfer assets to a separate affiliate without prior regulatory authority. The substance of every such dispute, however, is the exaction of a contribution to regulated markets.

In a proceeding initiated prior to the 1982 AT&T divestiture decree, a New York intermediate appellate court concluded that "The sale of advertisements for publication in the directories is not considered an essential public service." Nor could such advertising revenues be treated as "revenues received from the rendition of public service." *People v. Taconic Telephone Corp.*, 449 N.Y.S.2d 344 (1982). Unlike the other cases cited here, this New York decision was not reached in the context of a rate case in which the subsidy issue was directly involved. In the rate case context, however, the New York Public Service Commission adheres to the prevailing practice of appropriating "yellow pages" profits for the benefit of local exchange ratepayers. *Re New York Telephone Co.*, 74 PUR 4th 590 (1986).

38. *Separation of Costs of Regulated Telephone Service from Costs of Non-Regulated Activities*, 2 FCC Rcd. 1298, CC Dkt. No. 86-111 (1987); *Id., Order on Reconsideration*, 2 FCC Rcd. 6263 (1987). Summary versions of these two orders are published in 52 Fed. Reg. 6557 (Mar. 4, 1987), and 52 Fed. Reg. 39532 (Oct. 22, 1987).

39. This process has unfolded in what is commonly termed the *Computer II* and *Computer III* proceedings. The details of this complex history are not directly pertinent here. A useful summary, together with all relevant citations, is found at 2 FCC Rcd. 6284-5. See, in particular, *Third Computer Inquiry*, 104 FCC 958 (1986).

40. These carriers, as described by the FCC, "...do not attempt to determine their own costs..., but instead receive compensation that simulates the interstate cost study settlements that would be received...by a company that is representative of average schedule companies." 2 FCC Rcd. 6316.

41. The full text of these rules is found in 47 CFR § 32.27 (1987).

42. This is an example of actual disparate regulatory treatment intended to counter the managerial incentive to achieve the opposite result.

43. 2 FCC Rcd 6296.

44. For example, see *Re AT&T Communications of Wisconsin, Inc.*, 89 PUR 4th 85 (1987), in which the Wisconsin Public Service Commission adopted essentially the same transfer pricing rules covering affiliated interest transactions.

45. 47 CFR § 64.901 (1987).

46. *Id.*, ¶ (b) (1), (2) and (3).

47. *Id.*, ¶ (b) (4). For the currently effective amended text, see 52 Fed. Reg. 39534.

48. 52 Fed. Reg. 6558.

49. For a general overview and varying recommendations for the regulatory treatment of interaffiliate transfer prices, see Watkiss, "Utility Diversification and Federal Rate Regulation of Inter-Affiliate Transactions", 2 Va. J. Nat. Res. L. 1 (1982); Note, "Captive Coal

Pricing and the Regulation of Utility-Affiliate ", 68 Va. L. R. 1409 (1982); Note, "Using Market Bidding To Regulate the Transfer Price of Utility-Afffiliate Coal", 36 Stan. L. R. (1984); and Vondle and Ross, "The Regulation of Affiliated Interests", 113 PUF, No. 12, 32 (1984).

50. Ill. Rev. Stat. Ch. 111 2/3, ¶ 7-101, 102 (1988); Minn. Stat. Ann. § 216B.48 (West 1988); Pa. Cons. Stat. Ann. tit. 66, ch.21, § 2102 (1979).

51. Id., Ill. Rev. Stat., ¶ 7-101(3).

52. *Montana-Dakota Utilities Co. v. North Dakota P.S.C.*, 102 N.W.2d 329 (1960); *Application of Montana-Dakota Utilities Co.*, 278 N.W.2d 189 (1979) (South Dakota); and *Montana-Dakota Utilities Co.*, 632 P.2d 1086 (1981) (Montana).

53. Montana-Dakota Utilities Co. v. Montana Dept. of Public Service Regulation, et al, 752 P.2d 155 (1988). For an interim decision, see *Montana-Dakota Utilities Co. v. Montana Dept. of Public Service Regulation*, 665 P.2d 1121 (1983).

54. There is a suggestion that Knife River's competitive sale prices may have been more volatile, making exact comparisons more difficult. 752 P.2d 158. But *cf.*, 752 P.2d 161.

55. *Re Continental Telephone Company of North Carolina*, 56 PUR 4th 687 (1983).

56. *MCI Communications v. AT&T*, 708 F.2d 1081, 1116 (7th Cir. 1983) (citing J. Bonbright, PRINCIPLES OF PUBLIC UTILITY RATES 351 (1961); and A. Kahn, THE ECONOMICS OF REGULATION: PRINCIPLES AND INSTITUTIONS 150 *et seq.* (1970)). On the points of arbitrariness, economic irrelevance, or both, see also: Braeutigam, "An Analysis of Fully Distributed Cost Pricing In Regulated Industries", 11 Bell J. of Econ. 182 (1980) and Baumol, Koehn, and Willig, "How Arbitrary is 'Arbitrary'?–or, Toward the Deserved Demise of Full Cost Allocation", 120 PUF No. 4, 16 (1987).

57. CC Docket No. 86-111, *supra*, n. 38, 104 FCC 2d 59 (1986).

58. *Id.* at 67. Despite this latter day FCC disenchantment with its insistence on FDC methodology in Docket 18128, its order in that proceeding was judically affirmed. *Aeronautical Radio, Inc. v. FCC*, 642 F.2d 1221 (D.C. Cir. 1980), cert. denied, 451 U.S. 920, 976 (1981). Citations to the FCC proceedings are in the Court's opinion.

59. This brief characterization draws on the discussion in Faulhaber and Baumol, "Economists as Innovators", Vol. XXVI J. of Econ. Lit. 595-96 (1988).

60. For an example of the regulatory application of a stand alone cost analysis and "contestability" theory see ICC, *Ex Parte No. 347*

(Sub. No.1), "Coal Rate Guidelines, Nationwide" (1985) (Unpublished). For the basic presentation of "contestability" theory see CONTESTABLE MARKETS AND THE THEORY OF INDUSTRY STRUCTURE, 352-3 and 504-8, *supra*, n. 11.

61. 386 U.S. 237 (1967).

62. *Id.* at 244.

63. *Florida Gas Transmission Co.*, 47 FPC 341, 362 (1972).

64. *Southern California Edison Co.*, 59 FPC 2167 (1977).

65. 774 F.2d 1205 (D.C. Cir. 1985), cert. denied, 475 U.S. 1108 (1986). The opinion contains a more detailed history of the issue, including additional citations

66. *Supra*, n. 61 and related text.

67. *Supra*, nn. 63-64 and related text.

68. See: Columbia Gas System, Inc., American Gas Association 1987 Annual Listing of Constituents (1987).

69. *Re Columbia Gulf Transmission Co.*, 54 PUR 4th 31, 53 (1983).

70. The extent to which the putative benefits would be fully realized is, of course, a matter of controversy. See: Modigliani and Miller, "The Cost of Capital, Corporation Finance and the Theory of Investment", 48 Amer. Econ. Rev. 261 (1958). The authors contend that a firm's value and cost of capital derive from its flow of income without regard to variations in capital structure (i.e. source of capital). The theory assumes perfect market conditions, including the absence of differential treatment under tax laws of the deductibility of interest and dividends. The basic tenet of the theory is frequently ignored by regulators, where they fail to adjust relative debt and equity costs to the different risk allocations resulting from varying debt/equity ratios.

71. The following recent cases, culled essentially at random from the PUR 1987 Annual Digest, illustrate the process described in the text. *Re Alltel Carolina, Inc.*, 79 PUR 4th 305, 321-27 (1986) (N. Car.); *Re Wisconsin Electric Power*, 80 PUR 4th 31, 42-5 (1986); *Ex Parte Louisiana P.& L. Co.*, 80 PUR 4th 353, 362-64 (1987); *Re Pacific Northwest Bell Tel. Co.*, 82 PUR 4th 293, 325-55 (1987); *Pennsylvania P.U.C. v. Penn. Power Co.*, 85 PUR 4th 323, 384-92 (1987). See also: *Re New York Telephone Co.*, 74 PUR 4th 590, 612-15 (1986).

72. *Re Alascom, Inc.*, 81 PUR 4th 320, 357-75, 378 (1986).

73. 68 PUR 4th 396 (1985).

74. *Id.* at 410-11.

75. *Supra*, n. 36 and related text.

76. § VIII C. of the MFJ, 552 F. Supp. 231.

77. *U.S. v. Western Electric Co.*, 673 F. Supp. 525, 584 (1987).

78. Thus, the Court also acknowledged a "somewhat more amorphous risk" that the Regional Bells might "...neglect the relatively pedestrian, regulated telephone operations..." to concentrate on "...more glamorous...business opportunities...." However, the Court thought it "conceivable" that the FCC would address any problem of "substantial significance." *Id.* at 599.

79. It should be noted that in this same 1987 proceeding (*supra*, n. 77, at 597-99) Judge Greene gave blanket exemption from all decretal restrictions on diversification into "non-telecommunication" markets. The principal supporting consideration was the absence of significant common costs through which competitive services might be subsidized by cost transfers to regulated markets.

80. *Supra*, nn. 38 and 39 and related text.

81. Public Utility Holding Company Act of 1935, 15 U.S.C. § 79 (1981).

82. 15 U.S.C. § 79b (a) (3) & (4). Various exceptions of less importance to the present subject are found in these sections. Others will be noted.

83. *Id.*, § 79a(b).

84. *Id.*, § 79k(b)(1).

85. In a leading case the SEC was affirmed in its holding that the financing of inner city housing projects was not "functionally related" to the utility's gas distribution operations. *Michigan Consolidated Gas v. SEC*, 444 F.2d 913 (D.C. Cir. 1971). An electric utility was similarly barred from an equity investment in a cable television firm. *Mississippi P. & L. Co.* [1982 Transfer Binder] Fed. Sec. L. Rep. (CCH) ¶ 77,241. Vertical integration for gas and oil exploration has been allowed. *New England Electric System*, SEC Holding Co. Act Release No. 18,635, Oct. 30, 1974. For other decisions see D. Hawes, UTILITY HOLDING COMPANIES, § 3.05 (1986 ed.).

86. 15 U.S.C. § 79k(b)(1)(A).

87. 384 U.S. 176 (1966). See also: *Id.*, 390 U.S. 207 (1968).

88. 15 U.S.C. § 79c(a) & (b).

89. *Union Electric Co.*, Fed. Sec. L. Rep. (CCH) ¶ 79,751 (April 10, 1974).

90. Public Utility Holding Company Act Release No. 17201, Fed. Sec. L. Rep. (CCH) ¶ 78,155 (July 19, 1971).

91. *In the Matter of Pacific Lighting Corp.*, Public Utility Holding Company Act Release No. 17855, Fed. Sec. L. Rep. (CCH) ¶ 79,173 (Jan. 11, 1973).

92. *Id.* at 82, 573-74.

93. *Public Utility Holding Company Act Amendments: Hearings on S. 1869, 1870, 1871 and 1977 Before the Subcomm. on Securities of the Senate Comm. on Banking, Housing and Urban Affairs,* 97th Cong., 2d Sess. (April 27, June 8 and 10, 1982);

Public Utility Holding Company Act Amendments: Hearings on S. 1174, Id., 98th Cong., 1st Sess. (June 14 and 15, 1983); and

Public Utility Holding Company Act: Hearings on H.R. 5220, 5465 and 6134 Before the Subcomm. on Energy, Conservation and Power of the House Comm. on Energy and Commerce, 97th Cong., 2d Sess. (June 9, 1982).

94. *Id.,* Senate Hearings, 1982, 355.

95. For general surveys of recent and current developments in state regulation of public utility holding companies, see: Trends and Topics, "Diversification and Holding Company Formation", 115 PUF No. 6, 60 (1985); Trends and Topics, "Holding Company Formation and the Weakening of State Commission Authority", 121 PUF No. 8, 56 (1988).

96. 760 F. 2d 1408 (4th Cir. 1984); *rev'g Baltimore Gas and Electric Co., et al. v. Heintz, et al.,* 582 F. Supp. 675 (1984); cert. denied 474 U.S. 847 (1985).

97. This type of provision is the basis for jurisdiction over "holding company" formation in many states. While the holding company is not regulated as a public utility, relationships between the parent and its public utility subsidiary are subject to conditions imposed on the acquisition of control. In addition, regulatory authority over the public utility's affiliate relationships is another basis for a measure of holding company jurisdiction. An interesting example of these principles is found in *Peoples Energy Corp. v. Illinois Comm.,* 142 Ill. App. 3rd 917; 492 N.E.2d 551 (1986).

98. 760 F.2d 1425.

99. *Re Boston Edison Company,* 51 PUR 4th 145 (1983).

100. *Id.* at 150.

101. *Id.* at 157.

102. *Joint petition of Rochester Telephone Corporation, et al. for authority to effect a merger,* N.Y.P.S.C., Opinion No. 78-5, Case 27015 (March 27, 1978).

103. *Id.* at 10.

104. *P.S.C. of N.Y. v. Rochester Telephone Corp., et al,* 81 A.D.2d 200, 440 N.Y.S.2d 378 (1981); *aff'd, Id.,* 55 N.Y.2d 320, 449 N.Y.S.2d 463 (1982).

105. *Re Rochester Telephone Corp.*, 78 PUR 4th 335 (1986).
106. The stipulation offers no definition of "subsidization". In effect, the provision can be viewed as toothless or as an in terrorem disciplinary standard which could be invoked against any questionable conduct.
107. 78 PUR 4th 350-51.
108. *Id.*
109. *Rochester Telephone Corp.--Need for and Propriety of a Royalty*, N.Y.P.S.C., Case 28959, Slip Opinion (A.L.J. Boschwitz, Aug. 12, 1985).
110. *Proceeding on motion of the Commission as to the rates, charges, rules and regulations of Rochester Telephone Corporation*, N.Y.P.S.C., Case 29551, Opinion No. 87-12, Slip Opinion (June 17, 1987). (The textual statement, initially based both on published information and the absence of other published information to the contrary, was confirmed, as of July 5, 1988, by a knowledgeable official of the New York Department of Public Service.)
111. *Application of San Diego Gas & Electric Co. for authorization to exchange all issued and outstanding common stock*, California P.U.C., D. 86-03-090 (Mar. 28, 1986).
112. *Supra*, n. 109 and related text.
113. This conclusion is based on discussions with members of the California Public Utilities Commission staff and an attorney representing the company. Following an aborted merger proceeding with Tuscon Electric Power Co., San Diego Gas and Electric eventually accepted a merger proposal from Southern California Edison. See: New York Times, Dec. 1, 1988, p. 29, col.6 (Midwest Ed.) and Wall St. Jrnl., Dec. 1, 1988, p. A4, col.1.
114. *Re Southern California Edison*, 90 PUR 4th 45 (1988).
115. It seems correct to view these "Policies and Guidelines" as the product of negotiations reflecting staff expectations and anticipated Commission requirements which the company was ultimately willing to accept. This initial surmise was reinforced in telephone discussions with knowledgeable staff members and a participant in the hearings.
116. Wis. Stat. Ann. § 196.795, ¶ 5 (1987).
117. This provision appears to reflect an expectation (although not stated as a statutory requirement) that most nonutility affiliates in the appliance business will be located in the Wisconsin service areas of the utility.
118. As an example see Wisconsin Electric Power Company, 80 PUR 4th 31, 38-39 (1986).

119. In part from the growing recognition of endemic efficiency disincentives under cost based regulation, an effort has been made to "institutionalize" regulatory lag as a spur to efficiency. A New York experiment for this purpose is summarized in the FCC's Initial Notice, *supra,* n. 3, 2 FCC Rcd. 5213. See also: *Re New York Telephone Co.,* 74 PUR 4th 590 (1986); 77 PUR 4th 119 (1986); 85 PUR 178 (1987). In that the arrangement establishes a rate moratorium subject to adjustments for changes in specified cost categories, it seems to create a limited period of price level regulation. Another purpose of the arrangement is to avoid the need for *general* rate proceedings during the moratorium. The variety of issues left open for categorical adjustments, however, suggests that this particular quest for regulatory improvement is also not so easily achieved.

120. It is possible to view a standby charge as a price for one specific service (i.e., access to a system) and a commodity charge as a price for a another service (i.e., units actually consumed.) Thus, two part tariffs can present the complexities of the multi-product firm.

121. For discussions of multi-part tariffs and peak period rates see the following: (i) multi-part tariffs—J. Bonbright, PRINCIPLES OF PUBLIC UTILITY RATES 346-359 (1961) (non-technical); Zajac, *supra,* n. 22, Ch. 4, 37-40 (1978) (somewhat technical) and Brown and Sibley, *supra,* n. 18, 80-97 (1986) (more technical): (ii) peak period rates—The history of the so-called *Atlantic Seaboard* formula illustrates the problem. The issue involves the distribution of the fixed costs of a pipeline system on the basis of relative peak period or relative volumetric use. The FPC's original decision was *Atlantic Seaboard Corp.,* 11 FPC 43 (1952). For more recent major decisions dealing with formula revisions see *Consolidated Gas Supply Corp. v. FPC,* 520 F.2d 1176 (D.C. Cir. 1975); *Columbia Gas Transmission Corp. v. FERC,* 628 F.2d 578 (D.C. Cir. 1979) and these further FERC decisions: *Re Texas Eastern Transmission Corp.,* 51 PUR 4th 359 (1983) and *Re Great Lakes Gas Transmission Co.,* 54 PUR 4th 366 (1983).

122. This assumes the case where marginal revenue declines with output and where marginal cost (i) increases with output, (ii) is constant or (iii) decreases with output, but not as much as marginal revenues.

123. Where, as is often the case in a "true" natural monopoly, output expansion is accompanied by declining *average* costs throughout the range of demand, existing consumers should in theory be the beneficiaries rather than the subsidizers of added output. For reasons beyond the scope of this paper, however, regulatory reality does not always correspond to theory. A more obvious example is the

widespread negative impact on average costs of the expansion of electric generating capacity (especially nuclear).

124. Each of these weighting factors has been recommended by one or more parties to the FCC price cap proceeding. See: Further Notice, *supra*, n. 5, 232-241. (In particular, the sources of the statements on this issue by these parties are cited in n. 883, 233.)

125. Indeed, in this example, the firm could have an incentive to make the full 30% reduction even if Market B's price fell below marginal cost. *Infra*, n. 128.

126. This introduces a complication in the operation of the maximum pricing constraint. The constraint will apply to price levels rather than to revenue levels. Thus, more realistically, inelastic Market A is not likely to be totally inelastic. A 10% price increase may in fact generate only an 8% revenue increase. Nevertheless, in the example, Market B's price level must be reduced by 30% to satisfy the single aggregrate price constraint. The firm must assume demand related risks and will reap the possible benefits of these offsetting price level adjustments. For further discussion of the problem of demand (in addition to inflation) based adjustments see, *infra*, Chap. 2, B. 3. c.

127. For a further discussion of Ramsey pricing see E. Zajac, *supra*, n. 22, 21-32 (1978).

128. Assume that the price level constraint in Markets A and B is a weighted average of their respective prices. A price below marginal cost in Market B will decrease profits, but at the same time the aggregate index will allow the firm to increase its price in Market A. The Market A increase could conceivably increase profits by enough to more than offset any profit decrease resulting from a price below marginal cost in Market B.

This is not to say that a price below marginal cost in a given market (and, more generally, failing to achieve Ramsey optimality) will always be profitable for a firm under a weighted price index constraint. But an incentive for such a price may arise, depending on the nature of the weights, the price index, demand schedules and cost relationships.

129. See I. Vogelsang, "Price Cap Regulation of Telecommunications Services: A Long-Run Approach", (The RAND Corp., Manuscript N-2704-MF, Feb. 1988). This study extends the earlier work of I. Vogelsang and J. Finsinger, "A Regulatory Adjustment Process for Optimal Pricing by Multiproduct Monopoly Firms", 10 Bell J. of Econ. 157 (1979). For application of the proposal to two-

NOTES TO CHAPTER 2   PAGE 42

part tariffs, see I. Vogelsang, "Two-Part Tariffs as Regulatory Constraints," Mimeo, Boston Univ., 1987.

Important possible advantages of this proposal have been identified. The regulator needs only data that are relatively easy to observe: viz., the prices and output levels of each service and the firm's total expenditures. Since regulators would not be required to set the price for each service, the need would be eliminated for arbitrary formulaic allocations of common costs. The scheme could be implemented by using existing prices as initial prices.

The claim is made (and elaborate proofs are offered) that profit maximizing efforts under this particular price index constraint will lead in the long run to cost minimization as well as Ramsey optimal prices.

The difficulties of incorporating demand factors in price adjustment mechanisms (see, *infra*, Chap. 2, B. 3. c.) are suggested by the proposal's assumption of stationary demand. Absent the inclusion of some mechanism for demand related adjustments, the desired welfare objectives could prove elusive. The essence of the proposal, however, is to vest complete discretion in the firm to price in accordance with changing conditions of demand, subject to the overall cost based price constraint and index weights.

130. The following cases illustrate a widespread regulatory practice of allowing recovery of research and development expenses based on a record of *overall* productivity gains rather than on the productivity of particular projects or expenditures. *Re Connecticut Natural Gas Corp.*, 37 PUR 4th 287, 312-13 (1980); *Re Establishment of Alternative Energy Corporation*, 35 PUR 4th 290, 301 (1980); *Re Benefits to Ratepayers of Programs Conducted by the Electric Power Research Institute and Gas Research Institute,* 5 DC PSC 315, Formal Case No. 794, Order No. 8005, Nov. 21, 1984 (Digested, PUR 4th Annual Digest, 1985, 183-85) and *R e East Ohio Gas Co.*, 81 PUR 4th 434, 438-42 (1986).

131. For a view that the risk of non-recovery of "failed" investments in the circumstances of unduly low price caps may discourage cost reducing innovation see L. Cabral and M. Riordan, "Incentives of Cost Reduction Under Price Cap Regulation", Manuscript, Conference on Utility Regulation, Stanford University, April 21-23, 1988.

132. This problem might not arise if a marginal cost test were uniformly accepted by courts as the legal standard for determining predation. In major litigation involving claims of predation against AT&T, Courts of Appeal in two different circuits in fact applied, or approved the application of, a marginal cost related test. In so holding, the Seventh Circuit decisively rejected the use of FDC as derived

from FCC formulas. *MCI Communications Corp. v. AT&T*, 708 F.2d 1081 (7th Cir. 1983), cert. denied, 464 U.S. 891 (1983). By emphasizing the district court's holding that AT&T's pricing was above Long Run Incremental Costs *and* FDC, the D.C. Circuit was more equivocal on the issue. Nevertheless, a unanimous panel did note its "serious doubts about the usefulness of FDC as a measure of cost to be used in distinguishing lawful from predatory pricing." *Southern Pacific Communications Co. v. AT&T*, 740 F.2d 980, 1006 (D.C. Cir. 1984), aff'g, *Id.*, 556 F. Supp. 825 (1983).

The mild equivocation of the D.C. Circuit on the subject of a cost standard was escalated by the Supreme Court in *Cargill, Inc. v. Montfort of Colorado, Inc.*, 479 U.S. 104 (1986). From a survey of lower court decisions and economic commentary, the Court concluded that "Predatory pricing may be defined as pricing below an appropriate measure of cost for the purpose of eliminating competitors in the short run and reducing competition in the long run." As in *Matsushita Electric Ind. Co. v. Zenith Radio Corp.*, 475 U.S. 574 (1986), the Court in *Cargill* found it "unnecessary to 'consider whether recovery should *ever* be available...when the pricing in question is above some measure of incremental cost.' " *Id.* at 117.

133. NTIA Report, *supra*. n. 2, 6 and 68.

134. The rule proposal is printed and explained in Appendices "A" and "B", Oregon Public Utility Commissioner's Order No. 87-014, Jan. 7, 1987. The quotation is from then Commissioner Gene Mauldin's Jan. 8, 1987 transmittal letter to Co-Chairs Ron Eachus and Frank Roberts of the Legislative Interim Task Force on Telephone and Telecommunications Services.

The FCC is less eager to portray its "price-cap" proposal as a form of deregulation. That proposal must be guided through the shoals of a dubious Congress, aroused consumer groups and concerned competitors. To minimize public perceptions of a loss of regulatory protection, the FCC is content to characterize its proposal as possibly "...simpler to administer than the Commission's current cost-of-service approach." FCC "NEWS", Aug. 4, 1987, "FCC PROPOSES REPLACING RATE-OF-RETURN REGULATION FOR DOMINANT CARRIERS WITH 'PRICE CAPS' REGULATION FOR INTERSTATE SERVICES."

135. These provisions are in 49 U.S.C. § 10709, derived from the "Railroad Revitalization and Regulatory Reform Act of 1976", Sec. 202, 90 Stat. 31, 35 and "Staggers Rail Act of 1980", § 202, 94 Stat. 1895, 1900. A useful survey of decisional materials on "market dominance" is

found in Eaton and Center, "A Tale of Two Markets: The ICC's Use of Product and Geographic Competition in the Assessment of Market Dominance", 53 Transportation Law J. 16 (1985). For a subsequent rule amendment see *Product and Geographic Competition,* ICC, *Ex Parte 320 Sub-No. 3,* 50 Fed. Reg. 46189, Nov. 6, 1985. A recent court decision dealing with elements of product, geographic and transportation competition is *General Chemical Corporation v. U.S.,* 817 F.2d 844 (D.C. Cir. 1987).

136. A non-technical discussion of contestability theory with citations to significant market power literature is found in Bailey and Baumol, "Deregulation and the Theory of Contestable Markets", 1 Yale J. on Regulation 111 (1984).

137. *Supra,* n. 2, 53-55.

138. A more recent Department of Justice, Antitrust Division draft proposal ("Oil Pipeline Regulatory Reform Act of 1988") would join the deregulation of competitive oil pipeline markets with the initiation of maximum rate regulation in monopoly markets.

139. *Supra,* n. 6.

140. Title 30, Vermont Stats. Ann., § 227a(a) (1987). The provisions of this section also set out statutory guidelines for the board's determination.

141. Oregon Rev. Stats., Ch. 757, § 757.825.

142. Iowa Code Annot., Ch. 476, § 476.1 (1988). The Board's statement is in "Comments of the Iowa State Utilities Board", 5, CC Docket No 87-313, *supra,* nn. 3 and 5.

143. See: Lambert, "Bypass in the Natural Gas Industry: The Fruit of Regulatory Change", 117 PUF No. 7, 11 (1986); Howard and Westfall, "The FERC Opens Pandora's Box: Increased Competition and Heightened Antitrust Exposure for Electric Utilities", 121 PUF No. 5, 22 (1988); Pace and Landon, "Introducing Competition Into the Electric Utility Industry: An Economic Appraisal", 3 Energy Law J. 1 (1982) and Collins, "Electric Utility Rate Regulation: Curing Economic Shortcomings Through Competition", 19 Tulsa Law J. 141 (1983).

144. The problem of continued regulatory intrusion into "unregulated" competitive markets under profit level regulation is well demonstrated in the Illinois statutory provisions which seek to preclude improper cost transfers to regulated markets. Ill. Rev. Stats., Ch. 111 2/3, ¶ 13-507. Contrary to this predominant aim, however, the statute expressly forbids the Commission to "...allocate to any competitive service all *or part* of the value of investment in facilities utilized, or expenses incurred, in connection with providing non-com-

petitive services." (Emphasis added.) The provision calls out for interpretation as to joint facility cost sharing.

145. *Supra*, text following n. 123.

146. The FCC has tentatively concluded that practical considerations may compel the continued regulation of some competitive markets. In its Further Notice, the FCC decided not to attempt such market delineation as part of its "price cap" proceeding. "We tentatively decline at this point to adopt the suggestions of certain parties that this Commission free assertedly competitive services from direct pricing constraints....we believe that attempting to undertake such a proceeding simultaneously with the implementation of price caps would complicate the transition to this new method of regulation." *Id.*, 126.

The deregulation of particular markets has been the subject of separate proceedings. See: "Decreased Regulation of Certain Basic Telecommunications Services", *Notice of Proposed Rulemaking*, 2 FCC Rcd 645 (1987). This proceeding relates to certain "basic services" of "dominant carriers." Another extended proceeding was of more general scope. "Policy and Rules Concerning Rates for Competitive Common Carrier Services and Facilities Therefore", CC Docket No. 79-252. Its lengthy citational history is found at *id.*, 654, n. 7.

147. The deficiency could be also be exacerbated by inflation, or (absent obsolesence due to competition) ameliorated by investment reducing improvements in the art. The analysis assumes for simplicity that future changes in these factors are accomodated through the inflation/productivity formula. Such future adjustments, however, will not in themselves compensate for any past deficiencies.

148. An introduction to depreciation issues and related tax considerations is in Kahn, *supra*, n. 10, 32-35, 117-22.

149. Further Notice, *supra*, n. 5, 144. Two principal advocates of the theoretical utility of stand alone cost analysis had conceded the practical difficulty of its use in setting maximum prices for AT&T in its interexchange markets. W. Baumol and R. Willig, "Price Caps: A Rational Means To Protect Consumers and Competition." This was submitted as Appendix C to AT&T's Comments in this proceeding.

150. *Supra*, nn. 6 and 134, and related text.

151. The common understanding of these subsidy relationships is characterized by NTIA in these terms: 1. "...in some instances, the current price for basic exchange telephone service may be significantly below virtually any measure of incremental costs." 2. "We understand that current rates for local business services may approximate

incremental costs, while toll [i.e.interexchange] may substantially exceed costs." *Supra*, n. 2, 61, n. 80.

152. *Supra*, nn. 6 and 134, and related text, Order No. 87-014, Appendix "A", 3. Note that the differential would continue to be measured at the cost/price relationships as of the "date of election." Subsequent cost reducing efficiencies (or inflation/productivity changes) that might have altered the relationship are not included. In other words, the correction of the historical deficiency would operate independently from subsequent changes in revenue/cost relationships. The basic inflation less productivity factor was calculated at *local* CPI less 3%.

153. *Supra*, n. 127, and related text.

154. As applied to increments of the firm's total output, LRIC determination is a particular application of marginal cost pricing principles. In effect, LRIC represents the costs which would not be incurred if the firm's operations in the relevant market(s) were terminated. The LRIC of a particular market or product has thus been described as "...total company cost minus what the total cost would be in the absence of production [in the market or of the product]." Baumol, "Quasi Permanence of Price Reductions: Policy for Prevention of Predatory Pricing", 89 Yale L.J. 1, 9 (1979) (cited in *MCI v. AT&T*, 708 F.2d 1081, 1115 (D.C. Cir. 1983).

155. These issues are addressed in some detail in the FCC's Further Notice, *supra*, n. 5, 188-99.

156. *Id.*, 197.

157. *Id.*, 195-96.

158. For the telecommunications industry, NTIA recommends that the industry trade association (United States Telephone Association) and the regulators' association (NARUC) jointly develop a single national industry index. NTIA Report, *supra*, n. 2, 63.

159. The following are two representative definitions of productivity: "Productivity is a ratio of some measure of output to some index of input use." THE NEW PALGRAVE: A DICTIONARY OF ECONOMICS, Eds. J. Eatwell, M. Milgate and P. Newman (4 vol. 1987); "Output per unit of input employed." D. Pearce, THE DICTIONARY OF MODERN ECONOMICS (MIT, 3rd Ed. 1986). Inputs can be measured by cost or input units and output by value or output units. Productivity is often associated with labor input (e.g., output units/work hour), but its broader economic significance embraces all material factors of production, including capital, material resources and services.

The broad measures of inflation (CPI, PPI or GNP-PI) in themselves reflect the impact of general productivity in the economy. Thus, a firm whose productivity rate for a period is zero will nevertheless benefit from whatever productivity offset is built into the inflation rate.

160. For example, the FCC notes that between 1938 and 1985 the CPI rose at an annual rate of 4.2%, while its subindex for telephone services rose 2.25%. The FCC considers that this 1.95% annual differential corroborates other estimates of an earlier pre-divestiture Bell System productivity rate of 2%. Further Notice, *supra*, n. 5, 208-209. These gains under profit level regulation may be the result of regulatory lag incentives or a response to growing competition in various regulated telecommunications markets.

161. Noting that direct measurement offers the advantage of "capturing the exact factor sought", the FCC was more impressed with the "conceptual and practical difficulties" resulting in "the almost inevitable result...of debate and controversy." It further observed that "...much of the necessary data are not publicly available, raising questions about the ability of outside parties to review the calculations." *Id.*, 211.

162. *Id.*, 208.

163. The FCC has noted that BLS projects the publication of a total factor productivity index for the telecommunications industry during 1989. *Id.*, 213. Telecommunications, however, covers the broadcasting as well as the common carrier sector of the industry.

164. *Id.*, 213.

165. *Id.*

166. At a time when the so called "X" factor of the RPI-X formula was reported in Parliament as yet unknown, it was also stated that the firm's productivity gains for the most recent 5 years averaged 3%. 50 Hansard 1074, 1087-88, Dec., 1983.

167. For further discussion of this potential difficulty see *infra*, Chap. 3, B. 3.

168. The problem with any wholly automatic adjustment, of course, is its disincentive to efficient responses to cost increases. To the extent that the firm lacks feasible alternatives to the continued proportional use of the particular input, the automatic adjustment is justified. Otherwise, some special procedure for establishing actual cost impact may be warranted. See, Joskow and Schmalensee, "Incentive Regulation for Electric Utilities", 4 Yale J. of Regulation 1, 36-7 (1986); Kendrick, "Efficiency Incentives and Cost Factors in Public Utility Automatic Revenue Adjustment Clauses", 6 Bell J. of Econ. 299, 303-04 (1975).

169. The important issue of whether, and in what manner, a group, or "basket", of separately priced services should be combined under a single maximum price level, in contrast to maintaining a separate maximum for each separate service, is addressed in the next section on price structure.

170. Initial Notice, *supra*, n. 3, 5219.

171. *Report of the Director General of Telecommunications*, 1985, 9. The quoted statement is ambiguous as to whether the "volume of business" related adjustment would derive from actual changes in the preceding period or projected changes in the following period.

172. "Subadditivity" is discussed, *supra*, n. 11.

173. In considering the elasticity of particular markets, however, it is again necessary to distinguish between elasticity responsive to the firm's prices and elasticity responsive to exogenous economic conditions. For example, cross-elasticity among particular markets will likely differ in relation to these separate demand factors. Thus, where consumers have an effective choice between Services A and B, an increase in the price of A could result in a significant demand shift from A to B. In contrast, a general decline in real income may lead to a general drop in demand for A and B, or otherwise have a selective impact quite different from a price change in A.

174. See, generally, Chap. 2, A.

175. See the prior discussion regarding the firm's incentives to place a broad range of services under a single price ceiling and the possibility of resulting incentives toward inefficient prices in some markets. *Supra*, Chap. 2, A.

176. "To provide additional assurance to the low usage residential customer—for whom the exchange line rental can be a large portion of the total telephone bill—BT voluntarily undertook not to raise residential exchange line rental charges faster than *RPI+2* for the same five-year period." *Comments of British Telecom*, CC Docket No. 87-313, *supra*, n. 5, at 6.

177. These issues of price structure and relationships are discussed by the FCC in its *Further Notice, supra*, n.5, at 147-66. "Basket" is formally defined as "...that group of services, the weighted average of whose prices must remain below the price cap applicable to that basket...." *Id.*, 158. "Band" is defined as "...the range within which a carrier may raise or lower any individual rate element in any year and still be entitled to streamlined review." *Id.*, 161. Under "streamlined review" price changes require a 14 day notice, are presumed lawful and must only be shown to fall within the price level constraints. *Id.*, 176.

178. *Id.*, 158.

179. *Id.* Conversely, the FCC rejected "service-by-service or rate element-by-rate element application of a cap" because it would "...potentially permit pricing distortions between substitutable services,... unduly limit a carrier's pricing flexibility, and be excessively complex to administer." *Id.*, 157.

180. *Id.*, 163

181. *Id.*, 164.

182. Bypass opportunities might arise through cogeneration (electricity); through direct contract purchases of natural gas or electric power from competitive suppliers; or through the ability to utilize alternate power sources.

183. *Supra*, n. 146 and related text.

184. The redefinition of an existing service subject to the same continuing price would seem to involve the variable of service quality or quantity as much as price.

185. See, Further Notice, *supra*, n. 5, 182-85.

186. In some cases, however, new classifications will by their purpose and nature necessarily replace existing classifications. Marginal cost pricing proposals directed to peak period capacity problems may prove even more significant under price level regulation. The issue is discussed at *infra*, Chap. 3, B. 2.

187. Chapter 3 has two purposes. The first is to summarize in brief the major potential benefits of price level regulation, as derived from the Chapter 2 discussion of its incentive structure. The second is to balance against these benefits problems which might impair the successful implementation of a price level regime.

188. Initial Notice, *supra*, n. 3, 5211.

189. Further Notice, *supra*, n. 5, 33.

190. The problem of developing non-cost based standards for the oversight of price levels is discussed below. *Infra*, Chap. 4, A. 2.

191. Several problems discussed in this section were raised in in the particular context of the decisional alternatives that must be addressed in formulating a price level regime (*supra*, Chap. 2, B.). These are now addressed more fully and other problems not previously raised are discussed.

192. Major impetus was provided in the Public Utility Regulatory Policy Act of 1978 ("PURPA"), PL 95-617, 92 Stat. 3117. This federal enactment, in effect, required consideration (but not necessarily adoption) by state regulators of "federal standards" for marginal cost oriented pricing, including time-of-day rates, seasonal rates and a requirement of cost justification for traditional declining block rates. PURPA's constitutionality was sustained in *Federal Energy Regulatory Commission v. Mississippi*, 456 U.S. 742 (1982). PURPA and other major regulatory developments and decisions pertaining to marginal cost oriented rate design are discussed and cited in L. Schwartz, J. Flynn and H. First, FREE ENTERPRISE AND ECONOMIC ORGANIZATION: GOVERNMENT REGULATION (Sixth Ed., 1985), 770-829.

193. *In re Commonwealth Edison*, Order, Illinois Commerce Commission Docket No. 86-0128, April 27, 1988.

194. Issues arising from such preferential pricing (in this case for "elderly poor" consumers) are discussed in *American Hoechest Corp. v. Dept. of Public Utilities*, 379 Mass. 408, 399 N.E. 2d 1 (1980). For materials on the use of "lifeline" rates (involving lower unit prices for an initial increment of "essential" service) see Schwartz, *et al*, *supra*, n. 192, 764-66.

195. 583 S.W.2d 721 (1979).

196. *Id.*, 728.

197. 499 F. Supp. 53 (1980).

198. The underlying data is in *Id.*, Table I, 59.

199. 628 F. Supp. 1103 (1985).

200. For prior reference to the Vermont plan see, *supra*, nn. 6 and 140 and related text.

201. The elements of the Vermont plan discussed here are found in 30 Vermont Stats. Annot. §§ 226a and 227a.

202. NTIA Report, *supra*, n. 2, 67-68.

203. Further Notice, *supra*, n. 5, 251-52.

204. OFTEL'S Comments, NTIA Dock. No. 61091-6191, *supra*, n. 2, 5.

205. Report of the Director General of Telecommunications, 1985, 9.

206. Report of the Director General of Telecommunications, 1986, 12-13.

207. OFTEL Annual Report, 1987, 12. (A subsequent table in the Report (at 73) indicates a 1.2% allowed increase.)

208. *Id.*, 73.

209. Condition 20 of British Telecom's Licence requires separate accounts for the various businesses, and periodic accounting statements which show the basis for costs "determined by apportionment or attribution from an activity common to [regulated and non-regulated businesses]." Condition 18 requires the firm to record in its accounts at "full cost" any "material transfer" between the regulated telecommunications business and its other businesses. The same requirement applies to transfers to and from the regulated business. (Cf. FCC transfer pricing rules, *supra*, n. 41 and related text and Financial Accounting Standards Board Statements on "Financial Reporting For Segments of a Business Enterprise", *infra*, n. 228.

For a further discussion of British Telecom's accounting reports and cost allocation methods see *infra*, n. 229.

210. 320 U.S. 591 (1944).

211. *Id.*, 607. On the essential identity of the statutory and constitutional standards under Hope see also, *Permian Basin Area Rate Cases*, 390 U.S. 747, 770 (1968) and *Jersey Central P. & L. v. FERC*, 768 F.2d 1500, 1505 (D.C. Cir., 1985).

212. 320 U.S. 603. *Hope's* "end result" test as the measure of confiscation in public utility rate proceedings was recently and decisively confirmed by the U.S. Supreme Court in *Duquesne Light Co. and Pennsylvania Power Co. v. Barasch*, 109 Sup. Ct. 609 (1989). The central issue of the case was whether the State's disallowance of the costs incurred in connection with a cancelled nuclear project could in itself constitute an unconstitutional "taking" (or "confiscation"); or whether the impact of the disallowance is to be evaluated under the "end result" doctrine.

NOTES TO CHAPTER 3 **PAGES 79-80**

Of possible relevance to the subject of price level regulation is the Court's concluding dictum, derived from *Hope* and *Permian Basin* (*supra*, n. 211), that "The Constitution within broad limits leaves the States free to decide what rate-setting methodology best meets their needs in balancing the interests of the utility and the public." The Court had seemingly identified one such limit in this earlier passage from its opinion: "...a State's decision to arbitrarily switch back and forth between methodologies in a way which required investors to bear the risk of bad investment at some times while denying the benefit of good investments at others would raise serious constitutional questions." In combination, these statements may speak to both the legality of a price level regime and possible limits on arbitrary "self-serving" reversions to profit level standards.

213. In general, a diversified firm is protected against being compelled to subsidize its regulated markets by earnings from *unregulated* markets. *Brooks-Scanlon v. Railroad Commission*, 251 U.S. 396 (1920).

214. *City of Detroit v. FPC*, 230 F.2d 810, 819 (D.C. Cir. 1956); cert. den. 352 U.S. 829 (1956).

215. 188 F.2d 11, 15 (D.C. Cir. 1950); cert. den. 340 U.S. 952 (1951). The court was construing a "just and reasonable" standard under the District of Columbia Code.

216. For a recent application of the "zone of reasonableness" test, see *Jersey Central P. & L. v. FERC*, *supra*, n. 211, 1503.

217. *Supra*, n. 211, 797-98.

218. By its very nature profit level regulation requires that consumer protection at least begins with the level of the firm's earnings. Protection against "exorbitant rates", however, may not be limited to the earnings standard. It may be necessary to invoke the test where the firm operates at unacceptably inefficient cost levels, as measured by the overall costs of comparable firms. Such inefficiencies could lower the firm's return to the point of requiring rates deemed "exorbitant" even in the context of "normal", or even deficient, earnings. Protection against "exorbitant" rates resulting from generally excessive costs can thus serve as a complement to the regulator's disallowance of particular costs as excessive.

219. *Permian Basin Area Rate Cases*, *supra*, n. 211, 769-70.

220. See, *Farmers Union Central Exchange, Inc. v. FERC*, 734 F.2d 1486, 1503 (D.C. Cir., 1984). In this particular context, however, the court appears to equate the meanings of exorbitant rates and excessive profits. Its use of the quoted adjectives describing "rates" is

followed immediately by the statement that "Ratemaking principles that permit 'profits too huge to be reconcilable with the legislative command' cannot produce just and reasonable rates." (As for the required use of an earnings test under price level regulation, however, note the role assigned to "legislative command" in determining the relevance of profits.)

Farmer's Union involved the efforts of FERC to develop a rate of return methodology applicable to the regulation of common carrier pipelines (in this case of oil). Jurisdiction over this class of transportation carriers was transferred from the Interstate Commerce Commission to FERC in 1977. Department of Energy Organization Act, P.L. No. 95-91, § 402 (b), 91 Stat. 584 (1977), 42 U.S.C. § 7172 (b). As for Executive implementation, see 734 F.2d 1491, n.3.

221. The critical need for identifying issues likely to arise in the administration of long term relational contracts (the characteristics of which are present under a price level regime); for providing sufficient flexibilty to respond to changed circumstances and for resolving issues of interpretation authoritatively and efficiently are considered by Ian R. Macneil in a series of noteworthy articles. See: "The Many Futures of Contract", 47 S.Cal. L.R. 691 (1974); " A Primer of Contract Planning", 48 S.Cal. L.R. 627 (1975) and "Contracts: Adjustment of Long-Term Economic Relations Under Classical, Neoclassical and Relational Contract Law", 72 Northwestern U.L.R. 854 (1978).

Victor P. Goldberg has usefully applied these and other insights to an analysis of problems arising in the administration of regulatory contracts. "Regulation and Administered Contracts", *supra.*, n. 14. Related issues are considered by him in "Competitive Bidding and the Production of Precontract Information", 8 Bell J. of Economics 250 (1977).

222. "A decision maker who chooses the best available alternative according to some criterion is said to optimize; one who chooses an alternative that meets or exceeds specified criteria, but that is not guaranteed to be either unique or in any sense the best, is said to satisfice." Introduction to the entry on SATISFICING by Herbert A. Simon, from THE NEW PALGRAVE: A DICTIONARY OF ECONOMICS., Eds. J. Eatwell, M. Milgate and P. Newman (1987), Vol. 4, 243. The entry states further: "Faced with a choice where it is impossible to optimize...the decision maker may look for a satisfactory, rather than an optimal alternative."

223. NTIA Docket No. 61091-6191, *supra.*, n. 2, *Response by British Telecommunications plc to the NTIA's request for comments dated 10th October 1986*, 2. As previously noted, "Oftel" is the U.K. Office of Telecommunications, headed by its Director General, who serves as overseer and monitor of the firm's performance under the conditions of its license.

224. Interest arbitration is the use of arbitration to prescribe initial provisions of a new contract, or new or amended provisions in the renewal of an existing contract. It differs from "intrepretive" arbitration, which seeks to resolve disputes over the meaning of existing contract provisions. Use of interest arbitration in the United States is primarily as an alternative to the strike in the formation of collective bargaining agreements, and particularly in the public sector. For general reference to legal doctrines applicable to interest arbitration and citations, see: J. Weiler, Ed., INTEREST ARBITRATION:

MEASURING JUSTICE IN EMPLOYMENT (1981); Anderson and Krause, "Interest Arbitration: The Alternative to the Strike", 56 Fordham L.R. 153 (1987) and Howlett, "Interest Arbitration in the Public Sector", 60 Chicago Kent L.R. 815 (1984).

Interest arbitration is also used in the renegotiation of international investment agreements. W. Peter, ARBITRATION AND RENEGOTIATION OF INTERNATIONAL INVESTMENT AGREEMENTS, (1986), 75, 163-65.

225. The problem of improper delegation of legislative authority arose in connection with early efforts to use interest arbitration to establish labor contracts binding on municipalities or other governmental entities. In general, its use is currently considered as a lawful delegation where the governing decisional standards provide sufficient guidance for arbitrators to "write" contracts within the ambit of discernible public policy. See: 56 Fordham L.R. 153, 169-72 and 60 Chicago Kent L.R. 815, 821-23, supra., n. 224.

226. See, the debacle of the index in the Alcoa case, supra., n. 197 and related text.

227. Such comparisons would be further complicated by the impact of unpredictable technological change on service quality. In general, however, it might be thought that service reliability and technical quality might be valued more highly among consumers of basic core services than innovation in itself.

228. See, for example, Financial Accounting Standards Board, Statement No. 14, Financial Reporting for Segments of a Business Enterprise, Dec., 1976. See also, amendatory Statement Nos. 18, 21, 24 and 30. Financial Accounting Standards Board, ACCOUNTING STANDARDS, VOL. 1: ORIGINAL PRONOUNCEMENTS AS OF JUNE 1, 1982 and ACCOUNTING STANDARDS: ORIGINAL PRONOUNCEMENTS and CURRENT TEXT AS OF JUNE 1, 1986 (McGraw-Hill, 1986/87 Ed.). These Statements deal with the segmental determination of revenues, operating expenses, operating profits or losses and identifiable assets. With an allocation of equity to particular segments on a consistent and reasonable basis, annual changes in return on equity can be determined, as well as on recorded asset values. The key is in a reasonable and consistent application of GAAP principles, with any changes in accounting method and their impact fully disclosed for comparative purposes.

229. An example is found in British Telecom's accounts, in which separate segment revenues and earnings are reported. Revenues are shown separately for three main service classifications subject to the

RPI-3 price constraint, i.e., residential access line rentals, business access line rentals and "customers' calls" (covering all local exchange and domestic interexchange calls). Costs and profits are not shown separately, however, and total profits for the overall category of "Inland Services" includes the added service classification of "Apparatus", reflecting the sale or rental and maintenance of telephone and telex equipment.

For the year ending March 31, 1987, the firm's total revenues were 9.424 billion pounds. Profits before deducting 282 million pounds of unallocated interest charges were 2.349 billion pounds. In comparison, total revenues from Inland Services were 6.186 billion pounds, of which (omitting Apparatus) "RPI-3" services were 5.022. Total profits from Inland Services (including Apparatus) were 1.697. Profits on Inland Services in the two preceding years were 1.425 and 1.607, indicating a steady growth. Further details of revenues and costs are presumably reported to the Director General. The firm's Annual Reports describes its cost allocation methods as follows:

> While certain costs may be directly attributable to an individual service or supply activity, the majority of... assets and costs relate to the provision of the main inland telecommunications network. [These costs] are for the common benefit of all services which make use of it. Nevertheless, the group carries out an annual review to enable those costs that are not directly attributable to a single service to be allocated to services on bases *considered by management* to be appropriate. The attribution of such costs and of some categories of income is carried out by statistical apportionment and involves a degree of judgment. (Emphasis added.)

Annual Reports, British Telecommunications plc, 1987, 50 and 1986, 48. (This citation also covers the revenue and cost data.)

In preparing its accounts, British Telecom continues to use FDC methods. There are no obvious indications, however, that any resulting cost distortions serve as the basis of its pricing decisions. Whether its particular cost allocation practices have been questioned by the Director General is not known to the authors.

230. The "Guidelines" are in 12 CFR § 225.43, App. A. The Act is in 12 U.S.C. §§ 1841-50.

231. The extent of permitted diversification into non-banking activities is defined in 12 U.S.C. § 1843 and 12 CFR § 225.25.

232. See, *supra.*, n. 8. Condition 18 is titled "Prohibition on Cross-Subsidies". Its "full cost" requirement regarding any "material trans-

fer" between regulated and non-regulated markets is directed solely
to the avoidance of cross-subsidies to competitive activities. The vi-
sion of British Telecom as a newly privatized colossus engendered
substantial concern about its impact in competitive markets.

233. See, *supra.*, n. 228.

234. Reference here is to the New York and California proposals
for prescribed percentage royalties. *Supra.*, nn. 107-110 and 112-115
and related text.

235. In theory, the utility might seek to expand electric or gas
sales by offering to install free appliances for residential consumers
and charging its costs of acquisition and installation to all consumers
within the class. If the utility were operating on a sharp increasing
return to scale curve, the proposal might have some regulatory appeal, regardless of impact in non-regulated markets. Cf. *Cantor v.
Detroit Edison Co.*, 428 U.S. 579 (1976), involving a successful antitrust complaint by a retailer of light bulbs against an electric utility's distribution of "free" light bulbs to its residential consumers. If
the program were adopted exclusively by either utility, the other
could be heard to complain on both antitrust and regulatory grounds.
The complaints of electric consumers with gas appliances (or *vice
versa*) would be of price discrimination resulting from the inclusion of
appliance costs in the basic utility rate.

Under price level regulation antitrust considerations would not be
affected. The unique problem would involve the inclusion of appliance costs in the price adjustment formula.

236. This point is discussed in the preceding Section B. 1. of this
Chapter.

237. See, preceding Section B. 1. of this Chapter.

NOTES TO CONCLUSION   PAGE 98

238. *Supra.*, n. 8 and related text.

239. The issue of formula revisions to deal with possibly excessive earnings on inland services subject to the price level formula is discussed *supra.*, nn. 204-208 and related text. In this regard a British Telecom staff officer suggests that the firm's decision to waive allowed price increases at the close of 1987 did not reflect an effort to fend off future formula revisions based on earnings levels. *Supra*, n. 207 and related text. It is said to have resulted instead from a reluctance to raise prices in a period of service quality problems. The firm's more recent experience (from March 1987 to March 1988) suggests that as measured by basic standards of service quality those problems have eased. Performance improvements include significant reductions in the time required to complete installation and repair services; reductions in the time required to reach operators and information services; reductions in the rate of call failures due to defective equipment or congestion; reductions in the number of network faults per line per year (despite a small interim increase in the second half of the period); and an increase in the percentage of serviceable public payphones. British Telecom, Supplementary Report, 1988, 20.

Afterword*

A BRIEF SUMMARY OF THE PRINCIPAL VIEWS OF THREE COMMENTATORS

Professor Goldberg views price level regulation as an interim measure between more complete rate reviews predicated on actual costs. He predicts that these "regulatory lags" would be of insufficient duration to figure significantly in a firm's diversification decisions. He also contends that the "automatic" price adjustment mechanisms discussed in the book are inferior to more "hands-on" methods, such as "renegotiation" or "gross inequity" clauses. (These are viewed in the book more as last resort mechanisms for dealing with unpredictable and uncontrollable material cost changes.) In the case of diversified public utilities under a price level regime, he also questions the efficacy of efforts to regulate the firm's risk taking behavior in unregulated markets, either directly or indirectly.

Professor Phillips considers it important, in developing alternatives to rate of return (or "profit level") regulation, to identify the reasons for the "breakdown" of the current regime. In this respect he concludes that the authors unduly emphasize Averch-Johnson inefficiencies as the source of that breakdown. In contrast, he finds the main causes in (i) the macroeconomic environment (i.e., periods of high rates of general inflation and interest and escalating fuel costs) and (ii) rapid technological change. Thus, he suggests that even under price level regulation regulators will continue to rely on and tolerate the microeconomic inefficiencies of FDC (fully distributed

*See Foreword for reference to Commentators.

costs) "...to protect 'competitors' [in other markets] from the efficient provision of services by regulated natural monopoly firms." While not minimizing these and other concerns, Professor Phillips hopes that the authors' own "criticisms" of price level regulation "...do not lead readers to reject such proposals for regulatory reform." He concludes that "We ought not be deterred from attempting price level regulation because it won't be perfect—it won't be, but it at least has a chance of providing improvements."

Professor Pierce emphasizes the disparities between the theory and practical implementation of price level regulation. In theory, he finds that "Properly designed and implemented, price level regulation has the potential to eliminate the many significant and allocative inefficiencies that invariably accompany profit level regulation." More specifically, "[It] can create incentives for firms to set prices based on marginal cost and to establish price relationships reflective of economically efficient price discrimination." Nevertheless he concludes that price level regulation in the form being considered "...is likely to yield results less appealing than unconstrained monopoly or profit level regulation." He sees the source of the problem in the magnitude of the political constraints. These engender an "extreme skepticism" that any governmental institution could devise a regulatory scheme capable of satisfying the conditions required for successful implementation.

Professor Pierce is especially concerned about the likely inability of the regulatory process to establish economically sound initial price levels or price relationships through necessary changes in existing prices. His concern about the inefficacy of initial prices is heightened by doubts regarding the capacity of indexed price adjustment mechanisms to generate efficient prices. He notes that the mix of production factors is likely to change over time, often materially. The firm's own efficiency incentives will contribute to such changes, thus giving rise to increased disparities between costs and prices. He concurs in the need to consider demand factors in the price adjustment formula. But given the impermanence of demand elasticities, he doubts that any formula would work well in a "dynamic" market. He is similarly concerned that the identification of productivity gains from the substitution of price for profit regulation can be no more than a "wild guess". He also suggests that political pressures may compel the disaggregation of price ceilings to a degree that imposes as effective a bar to efficient price discrimination as "arbitrary and politically motivated allocations of joint costs."

Professor Pierce agrees that the potential advantages of price level regulation are reduced to the extent that firms perceive a risk that profit data may be used "at some time for some purpose." He concludes, however, that in practice profits will, and in theory should, be considered in determining the periodic ad hoc price adjustments that he believes will be required to compensate for inevitable defects in the automatic price adjustment mechanisms.

Professor Pierce is also concerned that managerial and regulatory incentives under price level regulation will militate against its ultimate success. In particular, he finds it unlikely that regulators will be able to keep firms from responding to their incentives to reduce service quality to large classes of customers. Conversely, the firm's theoretical efficiency incentives will be threatened and eroded by the powerful and largely unconstrained incentives of regulators to behave opportunistically. Professor Pierce considers that the success of any price level regime will depend on managerial confidence in the regulatory commitment to objective oversight. He concludes, however, that the conduct of firms will reflect the "little credibility" they attach to regulatory commitments.

The Authors' Concluding Comments

The main text and the comments reveal differing assessments of the likely success of price level regulation for the natural monopoly markets of both diversified and non-diversified public utilities. These differences should neither be minimized nor overstated, but their main basis should be understood. We believe that in large measure (although not entirely) these broad differences arise from a source of tension articulated by Professor Pierce in particular respect to the establishment of initial price levels. That is to say, can the political constraints on rational implementation can be overcome "...by meritocratic arguments based on appeals to economic efficiency."

In this regard two critical questions must be considered. Can comparative prices ever acquire sufficient economic credibility and political acceptability to reduce significantly continued reliance on profit levels as a prime measure of consumer welfare? Subject to satisfying fundamental social goals of service coverage, are regulators capable of allowing price relationships and their consequences to reflect market conditions rather than the artificial relationships and consequences of FDC (or their functional equivalents)?

Ultimately, the practical public policy question is whether the credibly identified potential benefits of price level regulation are or are not outweighed by these and other identified risks of implementation.

INDEX